INSTITUTE OF ECONOMIC GROWTH

Studies in Economic Development and Planning: No. 36

General Editor: P.C. Joshi

SLOWDOWN
Global Economic Maladies

SLOWDOWN
Global Economic Maladies

ANDREW BRODY

SAGE PUBLICATIONS
Beverly Hills London New Delhi

Copyright © 1985 by Institute of Economic Growth, Delhi.

For information address:

SAGE Publications Inc.
275 South Beverly Drive
Beverly Hills, California 90212

SAGE Publications India Pvt. Ltd.
C 236 Defence Colony
New Delhi 110 024, India

SAGE Publications Ltd.
28 Banner Street
London ECIY 8QE, England

Printed in the United States of America

Library of Congress Cataloging in Publication Data

Bródy, András.
    Slowdown—global economic maladies.

    Includes index.
    1. Economic development.   2. Stagnation
(Economics)   3. Business cycles.   I. Title.
HD82.B7236   1984   338.9   84–15040
ISBN   0–8039–2352–X

FIRST PRINTING

Contents

**Institute of Economic Growth, Delhi
Studies in Economic Development and Planning**

1. *The Role of Small Enterprises in Indian Economic Development* by P.N. Dhar and H.F. Lydall

2. *Indian Tax Structure and Economic Development* by G.S. Sahota

3. *Agricultural Labour in India* by V.K.R.V. Rao

4. *Foreign Aid and India's Economic Development* by V.K.R.V. Rao and Dharm Narain

5. *Agricultural Production Functions, Costs and Returns in India* by C.H. Hanumantha Rao

6. *Resource Allocation in the Cotton Textile Industry* by Dharma Kumar, S.P. Nag and L.S. Venkataramanan

7. *India's Industrialisation and Mineral Exports* by V.P. Chopra

8. *Taxation of Agricultural Lands in Andhra Pradesh* by C.H. Hanumantha Rao

9. *Some Aspects of Cooperative Farming in India* by S.K. Goyal

10. *Demand for Energy in North-West India* by P.N. Dhar and D.U. Sastry

11. *Some Aspects of the Structure of Indian Agricultural Economy 1947–48 to 1961–62* by P.V. John

12. *Wages and Productivity in Selected Indian Industries* by J.N. Sinha and P.K. Sawhney

13. *Inventories in Indian Manufacturing* by K. Krishnamurty and D.U. Sastry

14. *Buffer Stocks and Storage of Major Foodgrains in India* by A.M. Khusro

15. *Bangladesh Economy: Problems and Prospects* ed. V.K.R.V. Rao

16. *The Economics of Land Reforms and Farm Size in India* by A.M. Khusro

17. *Technological Change and Distribution of Gains in Indian Agriculture* by C.H. Hanumantha Rao

The books in this list have not been published by Sage Publications. Inquiries regarding these books should be directed to the Institute of Economic Growth, Delhi.

Foreword

This book by Prof. Brody is a major work. It deals with a subject of great concern to economists, to policy-makers and to the enlightened public at large in all parts of the world. Prof. Brody has been working on this theme since the early 1950s. The present publication is, therefore, a product of prolonged reflection stretching over more than three decades. During his stay at the Institute of Economic Growth as a Visiting Professor in the winter of 1982, the main theme of this book was presented by Prof. Brody in a series of well-attended seminars and lectures. The presentation was followed by lively discussions on the basic points of his thesis.

Prof. Brody starts from the fact that the world economy exhibited trends of uninterrupted growth and boom from the end of the Second World War and up to the mid-seventies. Thereafter, growth in both free-market and centrally planned countries seems to have slowed down and the rate of unemployment (openly in most of the free market economies and concealed or partly open in socialist countries) has been very much on the increase.

Many considered this slowdown in economic growth as a temporary malady that could be overcome by policy shifts. Prof. Brody presents a contrary view. He warns us that we should be prepared for a deceleration in growth, nay for universal economic stagnation over the next twenty years or so. 'Gloomy times are to come' is his dismal prognosis. He seems to suggest that the worst thing about the present slowdown is that there is virtually nothing that can be done about it.

The cycles not only operate in capitalist countries but also in centrally planned socialist countries. In fact, no system is really free from them. The message, as the very title of the book indicates, is not a cheerful one. What are the reasons, both theoretical and empirical, for this alarming prediction? It is here that Prof. Brody has offered fresh and provocative insights. I am sure these insights will be of great interest to specialists and to intelligent laymen, and that this book will stimulate a lively debate and also further work on this highly relevant theme of our times.

Institute of Economic Growth   P.C. JOSHI
Delhi   Director

Preface

It is easy to spot a mathematical economist: he spends most of his
day sketching graphs and scribbling symbols whose true meaning
only he can guess at; he will himself find them enigmatical after a
week or so. It does not matter: most of the fancy paperwork,
99 per cent or more of it, ends up in the waste-paper basket anyway.
Only a tiny fragment will see daylight, and then, of course, the
economist has to be prepared to provide a precise explanation of
the symbols he has used, clear statements of the corollaries he has
derived from his model, and an appropriate set of annotations. The
latter are supposed to enumerate all those scholars, mostly a handful
of kindred souls, who have already treated the problem or a similar
one, as well as to state how far his findings are in agreement or
disagreement with theirs.

It is cheap fun: it requires only paper and pencil and, occasionally,
a book, but only for reference. Even paper and pencil are not
always necessary: you can let your thoughts flow freely, to trace and
retrace their course, to divide and recombine, in the *camera obscura*
of your imagination, while gazing vacantly at the TV in the evening

or even at noon, while attending a boring meeting with a vague look on one's face and an empty expression in one's eyes.

Speaking about mathematics, people tend to expect it to be aimed at making numerical and quantitative statements, whereas the really important theorems have been always of a qualitative nature. For example: 'In a given economic system under such and such conditions, do or do not equilibrium conditions prevail?' 'When is the state of equilibrium unequivocal and when is it not?' 'Does a given system tend towards an equilibrium, and is it possible for it to reach equilibrium in a finite period of time?'

Curiosity, indeed, will not stop here. It will also try to adorn the skeleton of theorems with the flesh and blood of real data. This is the point at which mathematical economics suddenly turns expensive. It begins to make ever-new demands on statisticians, which, initially, are always considered impossible to satisfy; it starts to display a morbid appetite for ever more elaborate and more accurate series of data, for concrete numerical values. It then tries to feed these data into as large and speedy a computer as possible, teaching the machines to work according to the imposed abracadabra. Thus, the enormous amount of data is condensed and integrated into a few characteristic numerical values. Success is never sure because, in the course of computation, the fine mathematical theory may be found to have absolutely no practical value: it may be either perfectly unsuitable for computation or the result of the computation may turn out to be inaccurate and unreliable owing to the inadequate accuracy of either the initial data or the process of computation.

But even successful computations have their hazards. They may either correspond to already existing knowledge—in which case the research worker may feel proud, but his work will be void of new information, of any significant content; or the results might be in disagreement with existing knowledge and the author will have to face the really awkward task of deciding whether this noncorrespondence is due to the applied mathematical model, his assumptions, erratic data or mischievous computation, or whether (as happens in only a very small number of cases) it reveals an inconsistency upon which new knowledge and understanding may be built.

Thus, a mathematical economist may move mountains only to reveal a molehill. Only a person with enormous patience and perseverance will persist in this discipline. This book, for example, in spite of its relative brevity, reports on about thirty years of work. It was in the early fifties that I started discussing these topics with abler mathematicians than myself, mainly with the late Alfred Renyi.

The writing of the book itself has a history. Its nucleus was a short lecture at the Rajk Laszlo College of Economics, Budapest, in which, in the framework of a seminar about Kalecki, I compared my own ideas with his models. The first acknowledgement is due to the students of that college, their eager attention and criticism. The germinating idea was then carried to the United States where I worked for a year at the invitation of Professor W. Leontief in the inspiring atmosphere of the Institute for Economic Analysis, New York, and the Battelle Laboratories, Columbus. In the course of repetitions and reappraisals the originally quite short paper grew into a six-hour lecture course. It was presented for the last time in Puerto Rico, presuming on the patience of my professional friends, particularly Mr. Angel Ruiz, who sat through the lectures with the temperature above 40° centigrade.

Returning from the States, I was honoured by Professor P.C. Joshi, Director of the Institute of Economic Growth (Delhi), with an invitation to make a study visit to his Institute for a semester. It was a condition of the invitation that I write a paper on growth theory for discussion at the Institute. The discussion was attended by men of such distinction as Professor S. Chakravarty, whom I respect as one of the most knowledgeable economists of our time, and Professor A. Beteille, anthropologist and sociologist, who appreciated with friendly understanding how I was trying to extend the coverage of economics over fields that once fell within its scope of interest but had later been badly neglected and have since then been cultivated only as part of anthropology, demography and sociology.

Returning home, I began to mould the manuscript into its final shape. This gave rise to new problems. In some fields covered in the paper, first of all in that of the Kondratiev long-waves, new sprouts had sprung, while in other territories, such as on the fountainhead of productivity, new thoughts were dictated by the logic of the text.

With all my respect for the classical theories of economics and the eminent economists who propounded them, the views I offer are frequently at variance with and, in many respects, the opposite of generally accepted ideas. I, therefore, found it appropriate to give stylistic warning whenever my logical inferences became personal. The acceptance or rejection of sentences written in the first person singular (also of complete 'interludes') must depend on the credit given to the author. I do not imply that the train of thought presented in the usual impersonal way is irrefutable: indeed, more robust theoretical structures have collapsed in the course of the history of science. I simply believe that there the logic is self-supporting or evident.

As far as the ultimate message of the whole book is concerned (the Cassandrian prophecy of baleful decades to come for the old globe), I wish I were wrong and there were no need to face the gloomy prospect predicted.

Budapest   ANDREW BRODY

Introduction

Since the end of the Second World War and till the mid-seventies, the economic pulse of the world seemed so very regular and healthy. Yet, lately it has become arhythmic and feeble. From the mid-seventies onwards, both economists and statesmen have worn anxious looks but have nevertheless kept assuring the general public, with the optimism of a good doctor, that the trouble is merely temporary and symptomatic. The price explosion, the oil crisis, the growing contamination of human environment, the proliferation of inflation and unemployment and all the other distressing phenomena are but phantoms haunting the horizon of our discontent. The economies are not really sick; they do not show any organic disease whatsoever; and their supposed flu will be quickly cured by the usual tea-cure—hard-headed economic measures implemented by a political party, or a fundamental reform of economic institutions and of the rules of the game and the hoped-for revival will soon come; the sunny and powerful growth of the sixties will return.

The symptoms, however, keep multiplying and so does the number of pessimists who think that the problems are too deep-rooted to be

15

considered as merely transitional. In their opinion, we will have to face all the implications of a slackening or, eventually, even a complete cessation of economic growth.

In a previous book,[1] which was not widely current because of its rather involved mathematical style, I joined the latter group, a rather small one at the time, because I could not escape the theoretical inference that it was almost impossible to halt the continuing downtrend of the economic growth rate. This annoying conclusion is valid not only for the advanced capitalist countries and countries pursuing a planned economy, usually medium-developed ones, but also for the whole world economy. During the past six or seven years, the slackening of the growth rate has been felt everywhere— from the Soviet Union to North America and from Japan through India to Zambia—and there is mounting evidence of the need to make adjustments to meet the anticipated slackening in the foreseeable future; to accept not only the idea but also the fact and consequences of a minimal or zero growth, whether we like it or not.

Acting otherwise, we may find ourselves in the situation of a person on a dark staircase who, not seeing the landing, takes a big step into nothing. We would be very lucky if our lack of foresight costs us only a sprained ankle and not a serious dislocation.

I am prompted by this to try and present the trends in the direction of slackening simply and clearly. Alas, writing for economists in general today requires that mathematical reasoning be severely curtailed. But one cannot completely dispense with mathematics. It is impossible to scrutinize the connections and interactions among more than two economic variables in purely verbal terms and economic growth is determined by more than two factors even in the simplest case. When some economists persist in non-mathematical reasoning—as Ricardo did with respect to this very subject in his discussion of the falling rate of profit; or as Keynes did in his analysis of economic stagnation—they only bequeath enigmas to be disentangled by later generations. Purely verbal logic is not sufficient here, especially when one wants to

---

[1] *Cycles and control.* Közgazdasági és Jogi Könyrkiadó. Budapest, 1980.

discern not only trends but also orders of magnitude; if one tries to learn something not only about the direction but also the degree of expected changes.

For this reason, my argument will be arranged around a little mathematical model. The work of Kalecki, Harrod and Domar has made this model common knowledge among mathematical economists. It is sometimes considered to be a very nearly outdated and simple toy but it is nevertheless built on basically correct and fruitful ideas. It only needs to be demonstrated anew, derived anew, and its old parts scrubbed and reassembled piece by piece, to become a suitable instrument for grasping present-day economic reality.

The model was drawn up originally as an explanation and illustration of steady economic growth; but here we are going to discuss deceleration and a fairly unsteady rate of growth. Our discussion will cover the major transformations of the economy, its upward and downward swings and cycles, and particularly its deep-seated trends (those persisting longer than a generation). Precisely because of their long duration, these trends are well concealed and do not enter into the everyday awareness of any living generation.

The basic structure of this book is determined by its destruction-for-construction approach. The first Chapter, in which the original model is presented, interpreted and criticized, arrives at the conclusion that the model cannot be true unless it is given a much broader interpretation and unless the range of its coverage is expanded far beyond what its authors intended. This takes us to a broader definition of economic life than the current one and to different methods of measurement than the ones in current use.

Chapter 2 discusses the stability of the explanatory constants, the so-called parameters, figuring in the model. To explain means to reduce a changing symptom to its deeper and more stable cause. But what can one do when these deeper causes and characteristic 'constants' are themselves variables? One must obviously descend still deeper to trace the origin of these variations and to find the reason for them. In the course of this endeavour it will be found that, at present, all these changes, amplified by certain other traits, work towards a deceleration of growth which simultaneously induces other internal tensions as well, which are then manifested in a general disharmony of growth, in the so-called growth scissors. The relatively steady growth observed after the Second World War in several advanced capitalist countries is not an illustration of a universal rule but an exceptional and unique case limited both in space and time. As will be seen, even this smooth growth hid and accumulated internal strains.

Finally, Chapter 3 will discuss one of the very assumptions upon which the model was drawn up. A mathematical model is usually a mathematical equation and whether it will stand or fall depends on whether or not there is equality between its two sides. Here, the equation itself will be contested—even though contesting its validity amounts to questioning not only Keynesian economics but also endangering one of the greatest achievements of modern economic statistics: national income accounts. But the cycles of the economy are caused precisely by a basic inequality: the ever-present disparity between saving and investment. In view of the cyclic fluctuation, the emphasis will not be on the relatively short duration of investment cycles (which take approximately four years), the existence of which is more or less generally recognized by countries with both market and planned economic policies, but on presenting the longer swings, the so-called Kondratiev cycles, which take 40 to 50 years. The latest cycle, with its peak in the late 1960s and with all the accelerating recession that came in its wake, is substantially determining our path right up to the end of the millennium.

In the conclusion, a few ideas are mooted about the interaction of cycles, about demographic age-structure, as well as about the presumably not very rosy general disposition of the coming era.

1

About Growth

If Marx could describe his age as one in which wealth appeared as 'an enormous collection of commodities,' then, with some irony, we may claim that here and now this same wealth is pursued as national income, as a preferably big and rapidly increasing amount of per capita money, as expressed in statistical records.

And, indeed, the globe has become a vast racecourse where individual nations compete in respect of the magnitude and growth of their respective national incomes. The referees of the race, the statistical offices, measure and remeasure, summate and announce the achievements in each country—to be in turn further summed up and analysed by various economic integrations and ultimately reduced to an annual sum total by the distinguished and highly appreciated statistical apparatus of the United Nations, and published in fat volumes, causing acute storage problems in every great library of the world.

However, it is not the official bodies alone that pay enormous attention to this point; the citizens of every country are served (along with their morning toast, rice, millet, tea, coffee or infected water) with an almost perfectly updated report, printed and broadcast, on the production of incomes in various countries, about the progress of the 'production battle'.

The level of per capita national income and its annual growth rate is a generally accepted indicator of success. In this capacity, it has squeezed out all the other numerical or unquantifiable characteristics and has preoccupied the whole world so that every economic phenomenon is examined more and more in the light of its positive or negative impact on the development of this worshipped fetish of an indicator.

Figure 1 and Table 1 give some idea of the magnitude and the normal rate of growth of national per capita incomes. They are based on a detailed analysis by Eva Ehrlich,[1] and provide a summary illustration of the 'level of development' of a number of countries and the annual average increase of this level (depicted by the 'slope' of the corresponding column) as well as its total growth attained between 1937 and 1960.

The development of this indicator as well as, in a broader sense, economic growth and development, its qualitative traits and quantitative trends, will now be reviewed in an attempt to specify the ultimate determinants of this rate of growth, and to anticipate the growth path to be traced until the end of the millennium.

The Growth Rate

Having begun with the growth rate it is reasonable to assume that we know what we are measuring, we know how to measure it and are able to measure it accurately. These assumptions will get transformed into question marks of assorted sizes in the course of our discussion, but let us not pre-empt this. A logical-mathematical mode of discussion presupposes a subject which is accepted as such

---

[1] 'A Dynamic International Comparison of National Incomes by Physical Indicators'. *Közgazdasági Szemle*, January 1968.

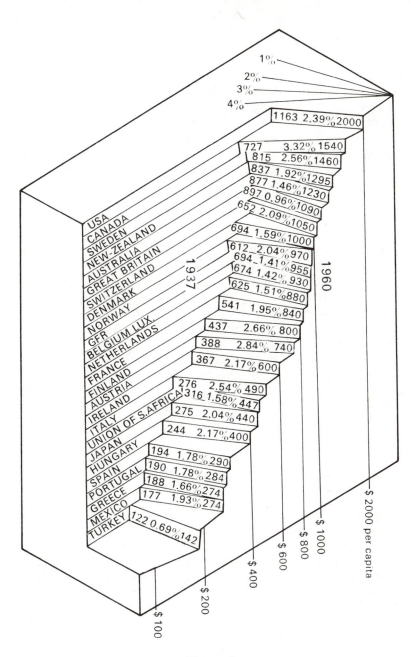

Figure 1

Table 1

Yearly Average Growth Rate of Per Capita National Income
from 1937 to 1960

Country	Per Capita Growth of National Income ($) 1960/1937	Country	Per Capita Growth of National Income ($) 1960/1937
Canada	2.12	New Zealand	1.55
Austria	1.91	Spain	1.50
Finland	1.83	Portugal	1.50
Sweden	1.79	Greece	1.46
Italy	1.78	Denmark	1.44
USA	1.72	Union of South Africa	1.42
Hungary	1.64	The Netherlands	1.41
Ireland	1.64	Australia	1.40
Switzerland	1.61	FRG*	1.38
Japan	1.59	Belgium–Luxembourg	1.38
Norway	1.59	Britain	1.22
France	1.56	Turkey	1.16
Mexico	1.55		

* Computed for the present era.

and which exists in reality. Therefore, at the outset, national income will be assumed to be something as palpable as the weight of a baby so as to make possible the derivation of reasonable inferences with respect to the process of its development—its getting fat or annoyingly thin.

How does national income grow? Economists usually agree that the bulk of national income is consumed and so does not contribute to growth. The remaining part which is said to be 'saved'—as it is not used for personal or public consumption—may be accumulated. If it is invested in new machines and buildings, used for the creation of new jobs or for furnishing old jobs with better and more up-to-date equipment, it will increase the productive capacity of the economy, and if this capacity is properly exploited, new, additional income will be produced. By relating this surplus to the original income we obtain the growth rate and so can speak about 5 or 10 per cent growth, or stagnation, or eventually about a 2 per cent recession. It is naturally imperative to specify here the exact period of time to which the change is related. However, the current consensus is to understand the growth rate as an annual or an annual average growth, unless otherwise specified. Now, it appears to be logically quite clear that the more we are able to save and invest, and the better the efficiency and productivity of the new machines, etc., the higher will be the absolute growth of the national income as well as the growth rate.

If national income is, say, 100 units and 70 units are consumed, 30 units remain for investment. What will be the efficiency of this investment? It will be equal to the additional national income it can produce. Hereafter, instead of this efficiency indicator (the 'productivity of investment'), its reciprocal, the so-called capital intensity, will be used. The latter shows the amount of stock required for the production of one additional unit of national income. If the capital intensity is 3 then an investment of 30 units of saving will produce 10 units of new national income and, consequently, the growth rate will be $10/100 = 10$ per cent. But if the capital intensity is 6, an investment of 30 units will produce only $30/6 = 5$ units of new national income and the growth rate will be only 5 per cent.

This amazingly simple and extremely logical reasoning (expressed mathematically in the so-called Harrod-Domar model) has two, only slightly different, forms. The first employs periodical, i.e., annual, variables. Here national income (let it be designated by the variable x), will be given an index k: x_k, where k stands for a given year. (In practice this may be 1950 or 1995 but, in a mathematical discussion, if the numerical value of the index is stated at all, the usual practice is to designate years by simple subscripts: x_0, x_1, x_2, etc., where zero may be a conventional initial year.)

If now s stands for the saving rate and b for capital intensity (rather generally accepted notations in international literature though some authors prefer to use their special symbols—symbols being like tooth-brushes, you don't like to use anyone else's), then the above train of thought can be conveniently summed up in one single mathematical equation:

(1) $s.x_k = b.(x_{k+1} - x_k)$

This equation may be read as follows: the left side expresses saving (the retained quota of national income) and the right side expresses investment (namely, the investment computed in terms of capital intensity and required to increase production in year k + 1 over year k). Thus the equation states that saving is equal to investment. This is one of the cardinal postulates in Keynesian economics. In fact Harrod derived his growth model from this very postulate.

As far as the solution of this equation is concerned (for as a rule there may be many possible 'solutions' to any one equation, depending on what you really want to know), if we wish to express the attainable rate of growth, it will be clearly the following:

(2) $(x_{k+1} - x_k)/x_k = (x_{k+1}/x_k) - 1 = s/b$

or verbally:

$$Growth\ rate\ = \frac{saving\ rate}{capital\ intensity}$$

Domar preferred a continuous notation. Here too, the variable of national income carries a subscript but usually an index t: x_t, this conventionally alludes to time being considered to be a continuous (that is, a non-periodical) variable. Finite increment is substituted here by the differential coefficient represented by $\dot{x}$, and since both the value of the function and the differential coefficient belong to one identical point of time the index t is often omitted in the literature. In this case x indicates not some unknown number but an unknown function. Another slight change is made: the propensity to consume figures instead of the saving rate, making up the latter to 100 per cent. Thus, when the propensity to consume is a, the saving rate will be $s = 1-a$. With these notational conventions the continuous form of the model will be

(1*) $(1-a)x = b\dot{x}$

and its solution, expressing the growth rate, will be as follows:

(2*) $\dot{x}/x = (1-a)/b$

In verbal terms, the solution is identical with the first one. Still, there does exist a little difference between these two results. The periodical model yields a yearly rate while the continuous model yields an instantaneous one. The relation between these two numerical values is exactly the same as between the simple annual interest and the compound interest of continuous capitalization. That is, if the periodical model shows, say, a 3 per cent growth, then the 3 per cent growth rate belonging to the continuous model actually indicates a year $e^{.03} - 1 = 3.045453395$ per cent growth. As will be seen, the statistical measurement is not accurate enough for the more realistic representation. Therefore, both forms are used in the literature and preference is given to either according to the possibilities and simplicity of mathematical discussion.[2]

There are two important corollaries to the mathematical solution, the first one being qualitative and the second quantitative. The qualitative corollary may be expressed as follows: *economic growth is of an exponential nature*. Given the growth rate $\lambda = (1-a)/b$ and some initial value x_0, the state at any moment of time can be computed by means of the exponential function in the following form:

(3) $x_t = x_0 \cdot \exp(\lambda t)$

Of course the growth rate itself is known to change in practice; it may either decrease or increase and, indeed, this is the crux of the

---

[2] The second model will be used hereafter. The form $(1-a)$ for saving rate lends itself to the analysis of the model in its multisectoral form, like the dynamic Leontief model. For the same reason it was decided to use capital intensity b, instead of its reciprocal! The matrix b of the multisector model normally does not have a reciprocal (or 'inverse') and therefore capital intensity can be used for 'division' only in an aggregated, single-sector model. This is one of the best arguments against the 'productivity of capital' approach, for there does not exist any extended, multisector form which may express it. The continuous form will be particularly convenient for the analysis of cycles.

whole paper. Still, having accepted, for a long time and habitually, the very notion of a growth rate and having spoken about the *percentage* of growth, by implication it is also acknowledged that growth is a process of this exponential kind and that the subject under study is the logarithmic derivate of national income (for this is the mathematical name of the value $\dot{x}/x$). *This* is what needs to be explained and not any other property of the function x. Explanation implies recourse from the agitated world of symptoms to something relatively more constant and it was not incidental that the growth rate became the recognized category of the process of economic growth.

It should be immediately noted here that neither the idea nor its mathematical expression in the Harrod-Domar form are entirely new. More than a decade before these authors, the same model was published by the Polish economist Kalecki who went still further in the mathematical analysis of growth; he was the first author to describe business cycles in a closed mathematical form.[3]

The origin of the idea goes back still further. E. Domar, who read Russian, mentioned in his first article that he met ideas resembling his own in papers of the Soviet economist, G.A. Feldman, who published a two-sector mathematical model of the dynamic growth of the economy in articles which appeared in 1927 and 1928 issues of *Planovoie Hozyaistvo*.

Here we have the first explicit mathematical formulation, but if we are not too particular about the mathematical form we may go further back in time. Feldman made it very clear that his models were of Marxist inspiration and, indeed, in the famous reproduction scheme of Marx, both logically and in actual numerical terms, though not yet of a mathematical cast, one can find all the main ideas and reasoning expressed in the Harrod-Domar model (and perhaps even in that of Leontief).

On its quantitative side, the information to be gathered from the

---

[3] His first treatise on this subject (*Proba teorii koniunktury*) was published in Warsaw in 1933 and was followed by many others until his death. His main findings and the first model of the business cycles was published two years later in English under the title 'A Macrodynamic Theory of Business Cycles'. *Econometrica*, 1935.

model is the following: the saving rate divided by capital intensity yields the actual growth rate. This conclusion appears to be valid, at least as regards its order of magnitude. The saving rate is currently in the range of 10 to 30 per cent in different countries, while the observed value of capital intensity is between 2 and 5. It follows that the observed growth rate will be between 2 and 15 per cent, a fairly accurate correspondence with the observed range of growth rates. However, the first uncertainty is already encountered at this point: in practice, both zero growth and decrease are known to exist. Capital intensity cannot turn negative, not even in principle, and usually saving is also given as a positive value. (Maybe the only exception was the rock bottom point reached during the big crisis of the 1930s.) Thus the growth rate could never be negative. Yet, considering all this, the information given by the model appears to be correct concerning its order of magnitude and so one may also tend to accept its implicit assumptions, i.e., that the only barriers to growth are the quantity and efficiency of investment.

It may be admitted that economists and economic politicians alike have generally accepted this inference and are thus apt to believe that the clue to growth has been found. The efficiency of investments is known to be determined by many factors such as the actual state of technology, the frugal use of fixed capital, better exploitation of capacities, and optimal distribution of investments among different fields of the economy. However, given a certain degree of capital intensity, and with capital intensity undoubtedly showing a slow rate of change, it does appear as if the rate of growth in any given country can be almost freely controlled, at least within the general bounds outlined above, through the proper setting or influencing of the rate of saving.

Let us, however, study once again the basic variables to which the rate of growth was traced back. Capital intensity is the first one. Is the value of this coefficient reliable enough? Is it safe to depend on it? I shall now briefly quote the conclusion of more detailed studies carried out elsewhere.[4]

[4] András Bródy: *Capital Intensity of Production in Capitalism*; and Jeno Racz: *Relationships of Fixed Assets and Production in Hungarian Industry*. Akadémiai Kiadó. Budapest, 1966.

An analysis of the capital/output quotient for a short period of time (shorter than the duration of a cycle of industrial production) revealed strong fluctuations. The reason for this fluctuation lies in the general state of business. Fixed property can be dismantled only at the point of its obsolescence or replacement and so it cannot follow the downswing of the business cycle. Therefore, in the short run, it is unreasonable to compare the *increase* of wealth with the *increase* of production because, sometimes, changes of the opposite sign occur: wealth may increase while production is actually declining and vice versa. The marginal coefficient correlating increments is totally uncertain.

Theoretically, the increments are correlated because increase of production in any one field of the economy plausibly requires the investment of capital. However, this theoretical point of view does not yield dependable and realistic results in practice, precisely because it neglects business fluctuations. The right method would be comparison at actual peak periods, at the heights of prosperity, at the fullest possible exploitation of capacities.

In spite of violent short-term fluctuations, the capital/output ratio nevertheless shows a rather constant magnitude. In the course of the period under study the ratio changed only slowly. Nor were any special international differences observed either from the point of view of the absolute magnitude of the ratio or the trend of its variation. So the behavior of the capital/output ratio is not affected appreciably by the general change of productivity over time nor its marked and simultaneous international differences.

The relation between national wealth (as an aggregate of reproducible real values) and national income displays a typical movement during historical development. The relation initially shows a (decelerating) increase and then starts decreasing. This movement takes place within fairly narrow limits. At the peak, following about half a century of the development of mechanized large-scale industry, usually around the turn of the century or a little later, the ratio is not higher than one-and-a-half times its average value. Nor is the ratio higher than 4–4.5 at the time of the peak (meaning that 4–4.5 of a year's national income is invested) and the ratio has not fallen below 2–3 in recent times either.

Since I summarized the above tendencies twenty years ago it should perhaps be added that, in the sixties and especially since the mid-seventies, capital intensity began to increase again slightly. The reason may be found in the higher capital intensity of automation, in the diminishing natural resources in extractive industries, the growing costs of preserving the environment and several other factors to be discussed later. Anyway, the observed increase of capital intensity falls behind the pace of the observed deceleration of the growth rate and can explain only a fraction of it.

So we possess a perfectly logical, almost incontestable and generally accepted theory. We also possess factual data which are not quite in tune with the theory from the point of view of their basic trends. The slackening of growth—which was by the way foreseen and taken to be natural by the classics of economics and which lasted till the turn of the century—may be explained in principle with the parallel increase of capital intensity. However, deceleration was not proportional to the increased capital intensity. After the crisis of the 1930s, capital intensity decreased while production kept stagnating for a long time and certainly did not accelerate. After the Second World War, at least for a while, until about the 1960s, production increased again rapidly, seeming, moreover, to be free from the big fluctuations of business cycles. However, its expansion never attained the speed that would have been expected by the decrease in capital intensity and all the efforts aimed at increasing the rate of saving. During the seventies, again, the growth rate started whithering away, which again cannot be attributed to changes in capital intensity or saving rates alone.

If a theory seems to be logically infallible and is still unable to predict the facts then the facts (that is, the methods whereby facts are recorded) are likely to be wrong. Let us, therefore, examine the methods of measurement, the theory and practice of computing and recording the growth of national income. It is not impossible that the disagreement between theory and practice can be eliminated through the improvement of the methods of measurement, i.e., through assessing reality with higher accuracy.

Problems of Measurement

The growth of national income was discussed above on the assumption that its measurement is a perfectly simple task yielding a sound result. Actually, however, measuring national income sets the statistician the task of carrying out an incredibly complicated and meticulous computation process. In real life, nobody produces 'national income'. What is produced is different goods and services. It is only the production and use of these most variegated products and services that can be statistically observed and measured.

The net economic output of a given year is obtained by subtracting from the new products turned out during that year all the old products utilized for and thus used up in their production—the so-called intermediate input—and then summing up the remaining part with corresponding prices. This is the 'value added' or the new value produced in the given year. These are then the figures from which the statistician must set out to compute the national income and all its sub-categories.

The simple model discussed above and postulating the equality of saving and investment becomes now extremely complicated in the colorful world of products. It is a vain effort to save muffins when the investment required in a given year calls for steel rails. For the smooth running of an economy, the equality of saving and investment must be true for each given product, and for each given branch and sector. It is thus apparent that a very intricate system of interdependence must be achieved to balance production, inputs, outputs, saving, growth and required stock inputs of each and every product.

Fortunately, the so-called dynamic Leontief model yields a concise short-hand formula and an expressive clue to this multiproduct generalization. Its form is identical to the model derived above, only the interpretation of the variables figuring in it is more general. It will be seen that this generality contains the earlier model as a special 'aggregated' case.

The basic formula of the Leontief model depicting equilibrium of economic growth is:

(4) $\qquad (1-A)x = B\dot{x}$

This is equivalent to the earlier equation (1*), symbol by symbol. However, here the symbol x stands not for a single variable national income, but for a vector variable comprising several components, including, consecutively, all the quantities produced of each and every product which may be measured in natural units. The time derivative of this vector variable, $\dot{x}$, expresses, as in the earlier equation, variation in time, i.e., growth, but again in vector form and separately for the growth of each and every product. Matrix B for capital intensities figures as a big numerical tabulation, indicating precisely those means that need to be invested for a unit increase in production. These data yield a fairly accurate estimate of the required investment once the targeted growth of production is known. This required investment must be met by the surplus or 'saving' of the respective products. The numerical table of matrix A shows current inputs required per unit of production of the same products, i.e., Ax designates intermediate inputs while $(x - Ax)$ expresses 'savings' or the surplus available for the purpose of accumulation.

If all the numerical tables and vectors are 'priced' according to the corresponding price system and added up then the value of x is made again into one single variable—an operation called 'aggregation' in professional terminology—and our detailed model is reduced to the former simple model. With respect to the growth rate, the solution will be *identical* to the result obtained from the Harrod-Domar model.[5]

However, the price system applied for the purpose of summation is crucial. Without giving mathematical proof, let us quote the thesis that error-free aggregation is assured if and only if the Marxian system of production prices is applied. This price system provides a uniform rate of profit on the invested capital.[6] It is easy to express

---

[5] A somewhat different interpretation of the aggregate variable x will be discussed later, after a further generalization of the model, and thus its meaning will be made as comprehensive as possible.

[6] See, e.g., András Bródy: 'Production Prices and the Average Rate of Profit' in *Problems of Drawing Up Input-Output Balances*. Akadémiai Kiadó. Budapest, 1962, pp. 211–5; and *Proportions, Prices and Planning*. North Holland. Amsterdam, 1970, Chapter 3.1.3.

this price system in a mathematical form as it is actually a 'dual' of the previous equation:

(5) $p (1-A) = \lambda\ pB$

Here p stands for the vector of production prices and λ for the average rate of profit which proves to be the dual of an equivalent to the growth rate. The left side of the equation indicates the current profit attained in the production of each product while the right side states that this profit is proportional to the capital invested. This generalized form is advantageous because it yields not only the attainable growth rate (and average profit rate) but also the *proportions of production* whereby this growth can be achieved, as well as the *price system* which provides the exact amount of profit required for the implementation of investments in every sector.

For simplicity, these proportions of production and this price system will hereafter be termed *equilibrium*. This equilibrium is actually an extended, multisector form of the Harrod-Domar equation spelling out equality of saving and investment. In other words, this detailed balance is already contained implicitly in the aggregate 'one-sector' model. Marx, too, expounded his famous schemes of reproduction in this equilibrium form. However, Marx was fully aware that, in practice, equilibrium is asserted only through its violation, periodic upsetting and periodic restitution. This very interesting point will be discussed only in the third chapter of this book which considers the implications of the violation of this extremely intricate and obviously fragile physical and financial equilibrium.

In the light of the aforesaid, it is possible to scrutinize the activities of statisticians in the course of measuring national income or, at an earlier stage, measuring growth of production.

Indexes of production are intended to measure the combined or common growth of different products, that lack any common natural unit of measurement, by dint of reducing it to an average value by 'weighting,' that is 'pricing,' the different components. The apparatus used for this purpose is the tool of statistical indexes. The problems and insufficiencies of such indexes are well known to expert statisticians. University students are cautioned in advance by statistical textbooks. Yet, professorial warnings are seldom heeded outside the classroom. Therefore, even professionals are unable to specify the possible or probable degree of their inaccuracy.

The point is that computing of a growth index, belonging to one single period of time requires two, usually different, price systems: those valid at the beginning and at the end of the period. By weighting the increase of production with prices observed at the beginning of the period, the 'Laspeyres' index is obtained, while the prices at the end of the period yield the 'Paasche' index.

The Laspeyres index used to be originally the most popular one and the prices prevailing at the beginning of some periods were maintained for considerable lengths of time. However, such measurements were apt to be overstated in the majority of cases. Janossy gives the following convincing explanation:

In the middle of the past century the price of aluminium was higher than that of gold. If, for example, the contemporary items of the Hungarian national product were weighted with prices prevailing in the year 1850 then, in the national product thus weighted, aluminium dishes alone would represent a higher value than total agricultural produce.[7]

The Paasche index computed with end-period prices yields a much lower rate in an overwhelming majority of cases. The differences between the two kinds of index are thus often marked, usually in the range of 10 to 20 per cent. There is a rather obvious explanation for this, of which an exact mathematical description was given by Bortkiewicz at the beginning of this century: the prices of products showing the highest rate of growth will, relatively, fall behind the prices of less quickly growing products over time or, in professional terms, a negative correlation exists between the *growth* of production and *price changes*. This was illustrated by Janossy: aluminium pro-

[7] Ference Janossy: *Measurability of Economic Development and a New Method of Measurement.* Közgazdasági és Jogi Könyvkiadó. Budapest, 1963.

duction showed extremely fast growth relative to agricultural production. The price of aluminium, on the other hand, fell relatively behind the price of agricultural products, supposedly because of growing production and demand.[8]

Of course, the contrary may also happen in economic practice. Moreover, in an era of state interventions such cases will multiply: if the production of any product grows relatively faster because its price is kept artificially high. In this case, correlation is positive and the Paasche index will stand higher.

For the reasons mentioned, statisticians tried to work with some average of the two kinds of index. The one most widely used is the Fisher index, a geometric mean of the two indexes. However, this approach implies that the 'true' price system and, consequently, the 'true' value of growth must lie somewhere *between* the values given by the two indexes. But this is not necessarily so and many economists question its very likelihood. The problem becomes evident in an extremely simple example making use of the theory of chain indexes and that of Bortkiewicz. Let there be the following sequences of data measured for the quantities and prices of two products manufactured through three periods of time:

		0.	1.	2.
quantities	q_1	10	15	12
	q_2	10	5	12
prices	p_1	1	1	1
	p_2	1	2	4

In keeping with statistical practice, quantities have been designated q instead of x, while p is used for prices. The example is so construed that, for the whole length of the period under study, the volume of the produced quantities should increase unmistakably by 20 per

---

[8] The same phenomenon could be explained also as follows: as a rule, production increases at the highest rate in those sectors where costs and, consequently, prices are depressed by technical development, making for mass production. Only such lower prices would enable the market to absorb the higher output of aluminium, e.g., for the manufacture of pots and pans.

cent, from 10 to 12 for both products. The expected index measuring the growth of production should be thus of the magnitude of 1.2. However, the value is powerfully distorted upwards by both indexes and, consequently, also by the geometric averages based on them. Namely:

Laspeyres index (*weighted with the prices of the beginning of the period*)

$$20/20 \times 36/25 = 1.44$$

Paasche index (*weighted with the prices of the end of the period*)

$$25/30 \times 60/35 = 1.43$$

Fisher index (*geometric mean of the two former indexes*)

$$\sqrt{500/600} \times \sqrt{2160/875} = 0.91 \times 1.57 = 1.43$$

Thus the computed rate of growth is more than double the actual value, whichever index is used. Hence it is evident that a rather wide range of uncertainty inheres in measurements of growth by statistical indexes. Strictly speaking, this cannot be termed an 'error,' since identical and absolutely unfalsified data, i.e., data assumed to be perfectly accurate,[9] yield different results to different statisticians if there is the slightest change in methodology or in the system of weighting.

As long as uncertainty and discretion, within given limits, are inherent in economic measurement, it will be safe to assume that the errors are not going to cancel each other, and that, as a rule, statistical organizations will take advantage of possibly uncontrollable discretion, and, let us say 'opinionate' allowance, to show pleasing

---

[9] Here it must be noted that even direct 'counting' cannot be perfectly accurate. Not, for the present, considering the imperfections of measuring instruments and even of simple counting, the original reckoning is always biased by real amd imaginary interests, resulting in deliberate misrepresentation. Although, with advance of civilization, culture and discipline, this range of error is diminishing, there still remains a critical limit to the accuracy of measurement. For example, if the number of workers in a factory is to be counted (a really simple operation backed up by the evidence of records), several pages of instruction have to be given to specify all the marginal cases (such as, workers temporarily absent, sick, on maternity leave, passed away, being replaced, etc.). Life constantly produces new marginal cases and it is impossible to foresee and codify all of them in advance.

results if at all possible. And they cannot be blamed because statistical offices are not private institutions, and their work 'certifies' the work of a government on which their budget, legal rights, and often the tenure of the officers themselves depend. It would be indeed surprising if they stubbornly insisted on reaching the worst of possible conclusions.

While emphasizing universal uncertainty, one must, therefore, also stress the tendency to overstate actual growth. Once again I rely for support on Janossy who, in the treatise quoted earlier, tried to break away from the traditional index methods and even from the use of price systems. His method was based on the governing idea that the proportions of the actual price systems, valid in the different countries and 'distorted' by various interferences of the state, must be neglected just as the exchange rates, similarly exposed to economic and political manipulations, should preferably be eliminated from statistical comparisons. He returned to the original physical measures of production and consumption because they can be stated relatively more accurately. Determining the most typical physical indicators of economic development, he could give a better, simpler and more demonstrative description of actual growth than traditional statistical indexes are able to provide. His methods of measurement, illustrated by Table 1 and Figure 1 in this chapter, have usually tended to diminish the official records of growth rates and growth differentials among countries.

However, there is a weak point in this method of measurement also and Janossy was perfectly aware of it. His method corrects errors originating from differences in national price systems and national statistical methodologies but the international average scale of measurement established in the statistical and economic routine is not improved; it is simply accepted as a reference scale.

In my opinion, this basic scale of measurement is also too 'steep'. It will be sufficient to quote Janossy who, in 1955, accepted 1700 dollars as the per capita national income in the United States. Among the figures given in this list are 61 for India, 56 for Belgian Congo and 54 for Burma. It is known that at that time the physical margin of livelihood (the 'poverty line') was in the range of $300 to

$400 a year, and this was naturally valid for the United States as well, measured by the price system of that country. But in an attempt to compare India and the United States from the point of view of development the data should have been recomputed on a common price system. It is impossible to accept less than a sixth of the physical minimum as a per capita national income in any country.

I visited both countries, somewhat later, when the computed values of their per capita national incomes showed a still wider divergence. I could accept that the average American citizen lives at least ten times better than the average citizen of India—although the difference shown in protein or textile consumption is not ten-fold and the difference in caloric intake is still less. Of course, we know that things like cars, washing machines or radio sets belong to the physical minimum in the United States, whereas they do not represent significant items in Indian consumption. However, the official list of per capita national incomes states a forty-fold difference. It cannot but be exaggerated.

Similarly exaggerated data are stated in national statistics. For example, official US statistics claim a more than ten-fold increase in per capita national income during the sixty years from 1896 to 1955, measured by the prices prevailing in the year 1929. But how could anyone live on $170 a year in 1896 if the physical minimum was over $300 according to the same prices?

So all these measurements are made along a scale which shows *implausible rates* of growth.

What are these 'scales of measurement' and what is the value of their 'slope'? Let us set out from the exhaustive work of Gilbert and Kravis.[10] This was the first study in which the production of the different capitalist countries was subjected to most circumstantial repricing. The differences among the countries were computed in three ways: according to the prices of the more advanced country which corresponds to a territorial Paasche index; on the basis of the prices of the less advanced country which is a spatial version of the

---

[10] *An International Comparison of National Products and the Purchasing Power of Currencies*. OEEC. Paris, 1953.

Laspeyres index; and finally on the basis of the formal international exchange rates, using official national income estimates as a reference.

In the comparison of, for example, the United States and Italy, the following values were obtained for the year 1950: The development of the United States was higher than that of Italy by 6.25 times according to the exchange rate; 4.75 times according to the Italian price system; and 3.33 times according to American prices. That is, the difference indicated by the exchange rate is two, or one-and-a-half times greater than the values given on the two other scales. In keeping with the international statistical routine this scale of the highest slope is accepted even by the Janossy method.

In a more accurate statistical measurement—which is naturally not always possible—the average of the Paasche and the Laspeyres index would be used and an approximately four-fold growth would be claimed. But can we take it for granted that the real difference is necessarily between these two indexes?

The traditional methodology of statistics, its whole theory, was advanced at the end of the last century when it was possible to regard the actual prices observed in the market as more or less 'unadulterated' prices, i.e., prices reflecting costs, supply and demand. But these prices of old times do not resemble the severely manipulated price systems of modern capitalism and socialism. Nowadays, the state budget cuts into costs to the tune of 30 to 50 per cent and, occasionally, much more, and then redistributes part of the spoils; then, through its skimmings, subsidies, restrictions and incentives, it will create such an intricate web of 'fiscal' costs that the price system is displaced from its traditional points of gravitation. What is more, economic policy usually assures higher prices for commodities whose production it wishes to promote for one reason or another. It is no wonder therefore if, all over the world, the quickly developing fields receive the greatest weight in measurement.

Let me point out here, as an indirect piece of evidence and as a new argument for the uncertainties of measurement, the procrastinating discussion about the activities that ought or ought not to be regarded as productive or valuable and thus included in the national accounts. I do not intend to contribute new arguments to this discussion, laden as it is with ideological problems and sometimes reminiscent of the debates of the scholastics; I would like only to review it from the point of view of the subject of this work.

In the West the 'value added,' created by banking, by the state administration and by all service activities, is deliberately included in the national income accounts even if the definition of the new value 'created' by these activities can hardly be correctly measured and even if it is secretly suspected that the increase of the administrative burden is not certain to add to the wealth of the nation, and may, rather, consume it. However, a higher than average growth rate is typical of these fields squeezed into the accounts and their omission would certainly reduce the stated rate of growth.

Socialist national income is measured in a different way. The tendency is to interpret physical production as narrowly as possible and to eliminate even such obviously valuable services as the forwarding of goods, commercial storage, communications, and many other infrastructural fields from national income accounts. The socialist economists have a secret feeling that, for the growth of material production, it is necessary to develop these fields as well. However, it is typical of these fields which are squeezed out of the accounts that they did and do show a slower than average rate of development and their inclusion in the national income accounts would certainly reduce the stated rate of growth.

There is a way to improve the precision of measurement which I feel is worth pursuing; but it is not an accepted way, and it is, moreover, in a tentative stage of development. At the beginning of this section, a price system was mentioned which is suitable for error-free aggregation, at least with respect to the rate of growth. However, this price system needs to be computed artificially and will be available only in such detail as is allowed by the available input-output tabulations. Therefore, statistical offices are disinclined to use it.

Nevertheless U.P. Reich made a daring attempt at computing West German growth data in this way.[11] His results only showed a

[11] *Allgemeines Statistisches Archiv*, 1979, No. 2, pp. 149–75. The computation was made for the years 1954–1967. Tentative computations were made with a similar

slight decrease as against the official statistics but, most interestingly, in the cases of 9 out of the 13 years, that is, in the overwhelming majority of cases, the growth rate computed this way fell *beyond* the range enclosed by the indexes of Laspeyres and Paasche. Since, in the statistical routine, these two indices *ab ovo* show a 10 to 20 per cent deviation, it must follow that the error of the statistical estimates of the growth index is at least as big and probably still bigger. An even greater uncertainty may prevail if the rate of growth is decreasing or low and at times of violent structural transformations (that is, if there are rapid changes in the proportions of production and in the price system). It may be therefore stressed that under the present circumstances, and supposedly also in the near future, statistical measurement must be considered especially unreliable. Its usual limits of error which, unfortunately, do not get due attention even in normal circumstances, have expanded to a dangerous magnitude and obstruct statistical clearsightedness.

It was U.P. Reich again who showed[12] a most awkward property of the usual methods of measurement: in an economy showing cyclical growth—as are the contemporary economies whose growth rates are usually subject to such periodical fluctuations—measurement might indicate growth even if, actually, there has been no growth whatsoever. Without going into a full mathematical review, this symptom is essentially due to the following cause: during periods of fast growth prices usually also increase, or at least they grow faster than in the declining stage of the cycle. Measured by rising prices the real magnitude of growth is thus overstated; while measured by decreasing or only slowly rising prices, the magnitude of recession is understated. It makes no difference if, at the end of the cycle, the economy returns exactly to its pre-cycle situation: subtracting the

---

method in Hungary too, but usually only for one given year or for the comparison of two countries and not for longer time periods. I mention only the names of Sandor Ganczer, Peter Glatfelder, Zsuzsa Daniel, Maria Augustinovics, Katalin Haraszti and Gyorgy Szakolczai, indicating that this method is not short of researchers and computations.

[12] Reich *et al*. *Arbeit-Konsum Rechnung*. Bund Verlag. Koln, 1977.

magnitude of understated recession from overstated growth, the statistical index may show a substantial growth—actually without the support of any additional real output.

In conclusion of this review of the statistical problems of measurement, let me say that the disagreements between model and reality cannot yet be said to originate from inadequate measurement. It has been found that though the error limits of statistical measurement are considerable and even disconcerting, the most important point is that these measurements are nevertheless suitable for the indication of cyclical trends of growth as well as for the comparison and monitoring of their changes. That is, the disagreement between the trends described by the growth model and the growth trends observed in reality cannot be explained away as resulting from errors of statistical measurement, however annoyingly big these latter may be.

Moreover, the analysis of statistical measurement reveals another important conflict between model and reality. In the first review of the model it had to be stated that the rates of growth as indicated by the model and as found in practice, or, more accurately, as measured statistically, were more or less in agreement and the general growth of the economy was really of the magnitude forecast by the numerical values, capital intensity and saving rate of the model.

But with the analysis of statistical measurement showing a universal inclination to overstatement and since actual growth is supposedly less fast than indicated by statistics, the inconsistency between model and reality further widens. The model may be seen to indicate an unfeasibly high growth rate since actual growth is much more moderate.

We have therefore to reexamine our model once again to see whether its explanatory variables really contain everything necessary to explain growth. Considering that the fundamental logic of the model seems to be perfect and hard to refute, the only alternative left for the reconciliation of theory and reality is a different interpretation of the variables of the model. Therefore, one has to ponder again: What grows when a country grows; is it the 'national income' of that particular country or perhaps something else and more important? Is the ultimate limit of this growth really the mere accumulation of means of production, machines and buildings or, eventually, something else not yet considered? These thoughts lead to another question: Is the quota of the national income earmarked for investment really the only means to trigger and achieve growth?

Let us scrutinize an actual economy where the limits indicated by the model are less pronounced.

A Zambian Interlude

A proud possessor of all the economic, mathematical and statistical theories discussed in the previous section but already troubled with some doubts, I proceeded to Zambia at the end of the sixties to teach growth theory and planning (rather, to teach what I knew or thought I knew about these subjects) as a Professor of Business and Economics. And in this section I relate what I saw there.

Zambia, formerly Northern Rhodesia, freshly emerging from colonial domination, set itself the task of industrialization. It has an area larger than that of France and a population about half the size of Hungary's; in other words, it is extremely sparsely populated. (Later on I learnt that, given the miserably inefficient system of cultivation, the available arable land was insufficient to meet the country's needs.) The population comprised of some 20 to 25 tribes of varying size, each of whose language was not, or was imperfectly, understood by the others. 80 per cent or more were illiterate, had never seen a school, and came from semi-settled villages or farms and pursued subsistence farming. Fairs, commodity production or exchange of goods hardly existed. Less than 10 per cent of agricultural production was sent to the cities which therefore depended on imported foodstuffs.

However, there were also about 30,000 miners who extracted and refined the ores of the country—and at that time the international market price of copper was extremely high, mainly because of strategic stock-piling. Therefore, through the prompt nationalization of mining, the government had practically unlimited funds at its disposal for investment. In some years the 'saving' amounted to more than half of the national income without laying any burden on public consumption (for, in subsistence farming the standard of living evolves in a direct relation between the tribe and nature and is hardly affected by any rearrangements in the lofty regions of the state budget).

Speaking purely theoretically, Zambia could have created as much as 20 or 30 per cent annual growth. Capital intensity was not high either; even basic manufactures did not yet exist in the cities. But the 'big leap' did not take place, growth ranged between 4 and 5 per cent a year and there were years when less than half or one-third of the ambitious investment projects were implemented.

How come? What happened? What prevented the 'absorption' of the major investments by the economy? Why did the grand plans prove abortive?

Well, in a fair percentage of cases, it was literally abortion. At that time there was only one paved road and a parallel railway in the country, but these connected it in the north with Zaire (Congo) which was in a permanent state of military emergency, and in the south with the totally hostile and still colonized Rhodesia (later Zimbabwe). All the expensive modern equipment had therefore to be imported through Angola and Tanzania; consignments were often bogged down in deep slush, arriving at their destinations after the rains, incomplete, rusty, or otherwise damaged. And even if the equipment was installed, there were hardly enough engineers to work it nor workers to operate it. After pay-day, the workers disappeared to drink, fish, or simply to visit relatives. It did not strike them that one has to work even if cash is not immediately needed.

I think the reason for this situation is clear: the missing element was know-how or, in conventional economic terms, advanced, sophisticated division of labor; a store of human abilities and skills linked with discipline—things which can be readily drawn upon in advanced countries, things available as a matter of routine to economic enterprises in industrial civilizations, thanks to a well-established and high standard of education and its specializations evolved over a long period in keeping with local conditions.

When I began to figure out how long it may take Zambia to overcome this disadvantage with regard to education and division of labor, I was deeply shocked. Even if all children aged 6 were immediately sent to primary school, it would be 8 to 10 years before the first generation which knew how to read and write, how to count and could orient itself to modern industrial life, would be ready to join production. However, starting, as Zambia had to, with unreclaimed expanses of illiteracy, it was also necessary to train primary school teachers at some high schools, and this would require another 4 or 5 years. Again, high school teachers would need some advance education which could be provided only by universities, adding another 4 to 6 years to this period of gestation now ranging to more than 20 years. And where would the university professors come from? At the time of independence, there were less than a dozen graduates in Zambia.

When all sectors of the educational system of a country are fully operational, when it is alive with students and teachers, we tend to forget how long it takes to get such a system primed and how long it takes to complete each cycle of training. An established traditional schooling system creates the impression of an abundant flow of new generations of ever higher attainment through all its channels to take over the burden and responsibilities of production from their predecessors. But when one is entangled in the problems of an infant system, one comes face to face with these 'delays,' often longer than a quarter of a century. For Zambia, it could take more than a quarter even half a century to overcome lack of education and division of labor through concerted efforts. And at the time of writing, the teaching staff in that country is still not totally Zambian. It consists substantially of transitory and expensive strangers, that is, persons hired from abroad. The proportion of such persons is slowly decreasing, but their absolute number is still on the increase.

And here growth theory makes a full circle and returns, after a long detour, to the classics. Long ago Adam Smith was convinced that division of labor is the 'clue' to development and growth. But then it follows that the production and reproduction, education and training of the working force, must be somehow included in the theory of growth. It is therefore untenable to assume that consumption (personal or public) does not contribute to the growth of any given country. Family care, health care and schooling are not only important in themselves but, under certain circumstances, become the dominating factors of growth. Let us now try to incorporate the findings of this interlude in growth theory.

Limits of Growth

If the growth model is drawn up as narrowly as was done by Kalecki, and Harrod and Domar, that is, when only the growth of the national income is studied, it will be inevitably found that only the invested, accumulated quota of the national income serves growth. In the spirit of the model, the maximum growth rate appears to be secured through investing the total national income, i.e., by curbing personal and collective consumption to the possible minimum or, if possible, even to zero.

We have here a strange paradox: though the ultimate objective is the maximal growth of national income and thereby of consumption, this end is seemingly best served by cutting the volume of consumption as much as possible now and postponing consumption to as far ahead as possible. This approach is in fairly exact agreement with the economic policy of forced industrialization essentially inspired by Stalin; always fighting against the 'propensity to consume' and warning, as it was put in Hungary: 'You don't kill the hen that lays the golden egg.'

This narrow-minded approach has proved to be politically mistaken and scientifically untenable because, firstly, it chases the rainbow of impossibly high growth rates; secondly, in addition to failing to state the real limits of growth, it practically eliminates these limits from everyday economic thinking.

Let us try to make at least a mental analysis of the growth not of bare national income but, more comprehensively, of the total metabolism of society: the full range of human activities. At the very outset we are in for a shock: all that is recorded in the national accounts reflects only a very narrow segment and a scanty fraction of the real activities of a society while it conceals an enormous and decisive part of it.

About 50 per cent of the population of the more advanced countries is gainfully employed, and only their work is covered in the usual accounts of national income. In less developed countries, this proportion is much lower. For example, in India, less than a third of the population may be regarded as gainfully employed. Assuming an average eight-hour working day and completely ignoring unemployment, this gainful work is found to cover only about 2,400 hours of the theoretically available annual time-bill of 8,760 hours, that is, less than 28 per cent of the life of the 'active' population. This means that, in the advanced countries, not more than 14 per cent of the total disposable time is taken into account. In less developed countries, this percentage is still smaller and, when total and partial unemployment are also considered, it will be less than 10 per cent. Owing to its apparent lack of productivity (because it does not create marketable values and is thus considered unsuitable for statistical recording), the remaining part—sometimes more than 90 per cent—is qualified as economically 'inactive' and is consequently totally disregarded.

But actually, even the time spent sleeping—amounting to 33.33 per cent of a life-time based on a daily average of eight hours—has to be regarded as productive because it is indispensable for the daily recreation of the work force. There are no economic or statistical records showing whether people in any given country get enough sleep and therefore go to work in a fit condition and high spirits or may be sleep only seven hours and therefore are morose and go to work in a state of nerves. Whereas this paltry difference of an hour is, in itself, no more than 4 per cent of the total time-bill accounted for, in terms of magnitude one may venture to say that happy dreams and adequate rest are likely to lead to a 25 per cent increase in the national income. Joking apart, let us put this as follows: by avoiding one hour of unnecessary loss of 'free' time through better organization of trade, transport and administration, *the same* national income may provide a 25 per cent increase in the quality of life.

This example in an extreme one, one of 'inactive' rest. But at least as much time is spent on household work manifesting itself in various services and products indispensable for the regeneration of daily life. Only when, in the process of an evolving division of labor, some of these household activities (such as, spinning, weaving, sawing, cooking, washing, cleaning, etc.) enter the market, partly or wholly, as production organized in an independent form, are they proudly recorded as additional national income. However, the actual output only increases if organized production not only continues to meet the human needs earlier met by household activities at the same level of satisfaction as the latter used to, but also meets them at a higher level of productivity—and there are many examples to show that it does not always do so.

To obtain an idea about the volume of work done and the technology employed in households, you only have to consider the highly revealing data showing that, in the most advanced countries (for example, in the United States of America), the value of the durable consumer goods used in households—they are mainly means of production: kitchen equipment, washing machines, driers, cars, mowing machines, etc.—is much higher than the value of equipment employed in manufacturing industries. In all likelihood, the situation is equally typical of the less advanced countries; only, the less sophisticated household utensils used there are not so precisely recorded because, being dishes, scissors, saws, etc., they represent smaller values and are only recorded as consumption of industrial articles. So it would not be surprising if, again in America, it turns out that only about one-third of the national wealth is owned by business enterprises and the remaining two-thirds is personally or collectively owned.

When accounting is limited to the national income, i.e., when only the exchange of goods sold in the market and labelled with more or less expressive prices is recorded, we must be grossly mistaken in measuring what actually grows and at what rate—and the requisites of real growth, the most important point here, are similarly misjudged. Consequently, the idea derived concerning the real limits of growth is a gross fallacy. I believe it is high time for us economists to admit our responsibility for the promotion of this false idea. Because we have artificially restricted the scope of economics to phenomena amenable to measurement, amenable to relatively simple accounting, we take note only of commodities sent to the market and handily labelled with (proper or improper) prices. And, as we have seen, even in this very limited context, we could not rid ourselves of serious difficulties in measurement. We are therefore not entitled to claim to have discharged the functions assigned to us by our fellow-men in our capacity as economists, and it is also very doubtful whether we approach the task in the right way.

In what follows, a more comprehensive view will be taken of the metabolism of society, its growth, and the limits of this growth. And here, again, we come across fresh surprises and find new orders of magnitude if the system of consumption and exchange of activities is drawn up in this broader context and we attempt to distinguish current input from investment as is done in the field of ordinary industrial activities.

Assessing all the inputs that remain invested for a long period (as in the channels of the school system)—that is, all the inputs invested in individuals for years and even decades before these individuals, as members of a schooled and trained workforce, are able to reproduce their original cost—it will be found once again that we are confronted with different, unusual and embarrassing orders of magnitude.

As mentioned above, the value of the means of production invested in the given productive branches amounts roughly, and on an average, to approximately the equivalent of three years of national income. Again roughly, the value corresponding to one year's national income is tied up in the *de facto* plant producing for the 'market' and about two years' national income represents the value of goods in the possession of households and communities.

Let us now try to estimate the multiple of yearly national income being tied up in the reproduction of the workforce (the 'semifinished product' of this 'production': the youth not yet mature enough to be productively active); and in all the educational, health, cultural, scientific, administrative and public services which are, directly or indirectly, responsible for training and organizing the workforce, enhancing its standard, usually in a non-market form, that is, in a form that cannot be expressed in terms of 'production' or 'national income,' or in any other form that can be accounted, but is nevertheless required for smooth growth.

Assuming that the economically active population is half of the total population and knowing that the other half is engaged in household activities and the reproduction and maintenance of the household, it may be safely stated that about half of the national income is spent on the reproduction, supply and maintenance of the workforce. For how long is this amount tied up? Considering the period needed strictly for nursing, rearing, and schooling, the formative period lasts from 14 to 25 years and it must be clear that during the past two centuries the time-span devoted to rearing and schooling has been steadily increasing and, moreover, an increasing share of the workforce receives a relatively longer schooling at high schools, colleges, and universities. With the historic abolition of child labor and the introduction of compulsory public education, the multiple of national income tied up in these fields is thus not less than 7. So, already at this early point, it is more than double the value tied up in means of production and already at least seven times the amount devoted to actual production for the market, the latter tying up, as stated earlier, only about one year's national income. Further, the value tied up in the workforce has been and is still constantly growing, with respect to both its absolute magnitude and in relation to the stock fixed in the apparatus of market production.

Considering, further, the not insignificant and steadily increasing part of the economically active population engaged in imparting, maintaining, extending and refining knowledge and culture in institutions ranging from research institutes to schools, from municipalities and offices through health organizations to cultural institutions, it becomes quite clear that the vast wealth inherent in the knowledge, skills, culture and working ability of the population is still badly underestimated. Abbot Galiani, a mercantilist of the eighteenth century, was perfectly right when he said: 'The real wealth...is man.'[13]

Now, if the potential accumulated in the workforce is the dominating one among the given resources of society, then, evidently, this will determine the ultimate degree and rate of growth, irrespective of the fact that its precise assessment has hardly been attempted so far, and irrespective of whether or not it is amenable to measurement or expression in numerical terms.

Lacking dependable statistics, it is of course impossible today to implement a numerical model in this generalized form. However, its spirit is yielding correct guidance and the analysis can be carried further in the direction of the influence of these more comprehensive relations upon the rate of growth.

However, this growth also now manifests itself beyond the narrow concept of national income, a category that has turned out to be too restricted to measure the activity of a society. The vector x, aggregated to one single numerical value, is no longer an index of national income alone. It comprises the level of the whole economic activity, and not only that of productive and service activities but also of activities observed in the reproduction, schooling and training of the workforce. If we can ever formulate it statistically, its value will be much greater than that of the national income, greater than that of gross national production, and will surpass even the value of aggregated social production. Statistics concerning education and training are already available but they are far from being adequate because the index number sought for must cover all human activities, including those required for the reproduction of the workforce, the households and even of human life. In this respect, the 'volumes' of the primary physical units are yet hardly recorded, though some data are already available from demographic accounts, household statistics and sociological questionnaires. The assessing, 'pricing' or 'weighing' of these activities will foreseeably raise tough problems. But this should not scare us away. It should be noted that the subject of Home Economics is already integrated in economic tuition in the

---

[13] Galiani: *Della Moneta*. Custodi, Vol. III, p. 229.

United States and although its prime objective is to spread the know-how of housekeeping and to study the rationalization of household work, it nevertheless advances at a deliberate and steady pace towards exploring and assessing household data and coupling them with economic statistics and national economic accounts.

I am convinced that this broader range measurement is basically a feasible task. Before the early attempts to draw up national accounts, the reckoning of national income had not been more promising or easier or better suited to numerical manipulation. The problem of assessing the national wealth is still to be satisfactorily solved and its computation is as yet not too reliable a field of statistical work. Assessment now ought to proceed to the assessment of the workforce for, as I argued above, till now only 5 to 10 per cent of human activities are recorded in a close and satisfactory order. The lion's share of the work is yet to be done.

From this broader outlook, it is clear that the economic strategy of forced industrialization was basically wrong. When one concentrates on increasing the national income and tries to rapidly increase the production of the basic material sectors through applying relative restrictions on consumption, growth will take place to the detriment of the enhanced reproduction of the workforce and, consequently, it will deplete the ultimate resources of growth. Some mistakes of this economic policy have already been recognized and there have been a few initial steps in industrializing economies to make up for the under-development of services and infrastructural branches. It has been realized for example that such activities are indispensable for providing a better supply of workforce and for the easy organization of economic life, no matter what market value may be attached to it. But we are still far from directing our efforts to expanding the real and ultimate resource of growth or even to acknowledging the not insignificant shift in proportions and emphasis this would require. That is why I believe the latest western economic policy, marked by the name of Milton Friedman in theory and by Margaret Thatcher and Ronald Reagan in practice, to be extremely retrogressive. In the grip of slackening growth they hope to find a solution by trimming educational, health, and welfare budgets. In this manner they do incredible harm not only to the sources of future growth but also to the disposition of the immediate future. Such 'solutions' should not be branded as medieval because this would only insult the Middle Ages. It is well known that in medieval times much greater importance was attributed to the polishing of human intellect and, indeed, there could have been no modern development in Europe without this deep respect for education, a respect now sadly absent.

2

About Deceleration

Our review of the theoretical and statistical procedure followed to measure growth has shown that all growth achievements have been drastically over-estimated because, so far, attention has been focused on a very narrow range of symptoms, namely, on variables that, besides being measurable, indicated relatively fast growth in the past. It is, of course, true that much has been achieved since the industrial revolution, but these achievements appear less significant if estimated on the basis of the total activity of the society and not only on the part covered in statistical reports. Taking note of fields not considered or measured in statistical reports, which always grew at a much slower rate (their growth being retarded and occasionally even reversed), may give us the strength to face current and future sluggishness in the growth of our prided per capita national income.

Casting doubt on inflated growth reports does not imply denigration of growth as such, let alone of development. Nor does it imply a belittling of the achievements of different countries or the differences between their respective levels of development. It is merely a warning that the scale of measurement over-rates the absolute levels achieved. But if relative distances are considered and one country is found to be lagging 20 or 30 years behind another, or if the division of labor in a given country follows patterns that were prevalent in currently advanced countries 100 or 150 years ago, as measured by the structure of employment, these statements will still hold because they are independent of the slope of the measuring scale. Decreasing the slope only implies that growth will be slower. Even if the average growth rate is actually only 1 to 2 per cent a year instead of the signalled 3 or 4, Uganda will still lag 100–200 years in terms of development behind Switzerland and it is scanty satisfaction to observe that the difference between the per capita national incomes, presently over fifty-fold (4 per cent per annum for 100 years) may be 'reduced' to seven-fold (with 2 per cent for 100 years). It will still need the same 100 or 200 years to cover this 'shorter distance'. With a yearly average of 1 per cent growth, per capita national income is multiplied only 2.7 times over 100 years; however, this similarly requires the efforts of the same 100 years, except that it is now measured on a scale that is less steep and therefore closer to real life.

But all this is only an imaginary deceleration of growth. If you scaled a peak under the impression that you were climbing ten thousand feet only to find out later that it measures only six thousand feet, you may be a little upset but may still be proud of climbing higher than others who believe they are seven thousand feet high, though more accurate measurement indicates that they have reached only three thousand feet. But there is also another, non-fictive deceleration of growth which does not depend on the scale of measurement or on the methods of measurement adopted and which had been noticed earlier by classical economists like Smith, Ricardo and Marx at the time of rising industrialization. The point they made was that a drop in the profit rate is simply another expression for a drop in the growth rate, the rate of capital accumulation being ultimately determined by the attained profit and its rate.

The Classical Analysis

For the classical economists, the declining rate of profit was an empirical fact whose existence was taken for granted. Their investigation sought to uncover its cause and did not question its existence or degree. However, it is not impossible that the observed downtrend, or at least part of it, may have been illusory.

As commodity production unfolds, the accompanying surge of production may be partly illusory because the mere transformation of products, traditionally turned out by the family or the village community, into items of exchange does not, in itself, necessarily imply augmented production. Since in statistics only commodity production and not production itself is measured, much of the growth recorded in such periods is not growth but a mere metamorphosis: products becoming merchandise. With the spread of industrialization, labor itself also becomes a commodity, though it has been seen that the creation of a workforce is statistically not regarded as part of either commodity production or of national production.

Now industrialization first takes control of areas easily and quickly penetrable; only later, and much more slowly, does it intrude into less hospitable domains. There still exist areas of human activity which remain partly or absolutely out of bounds, even in the most advanced capitalist countries. The slowdown in the unfolding process of ever-new branches, services and activities being brought under the control of the market indicates the inevitable slow exhaustion of the territory available for occupation and signals the saturation point of only a specific mode of production: commodity production. It does not necessarily indicate a slackening in the pace of human activities and production in general.

Therefore, the declining rate of capitalist profit in the fields cultivated by capital is compatible with a steady growth of total production—at least as long as the overwhelming majority of production is not dominated by capitalist production. This happened in western Europe only at the end of the nineteenth century because only then did the overwhelming majority of labor become wage-labor. This explains the apparent inconsistency between the classical ideas and the growth statistics[1] compiled nowadays. The classical economists used to concentrate their full attention on capitalist production whereas statistics record the rate of *commodity* production.

There is another, though less significant, reason why the profit rate may have appeared to be falling, namely, the invention of taxes on profit creating all the fraudulence accompanying tax returns, individual evasion of taxation and the various forms of tax fraud. It is nevertheless probable that a real decline in the profit rate, along with a declining growth rate of production, was at least partially a very real symptom. Smith, and later on Ricardo, supposed it to be due to the diminishing returns of agricultural production. With increasing production and population, production was carried to less and less fertile agricultural areas. As a result of the reclamation of new land, the absolute volume of additional produce was augmented but, as a result of decreasing productivity, production required relatively higher current and capital outlays and this entailed a shrinking profit rate.

This reasoning, however, leads to a contradiction. The classical economist derived land rent from differences in the fertility of cultivated land. If one assumes that production involves less and less fertile areas then the differential fertility must increase and so must land rent, both absolutely and relatively. But it was impossible to show a relative increase in land rents (their actual share declined) and therefore this explanation was completely discarded by Marx.

It does not belong to the subject of this work to review the more sophisticated theory of land rents, although both the Marxian theory and Georgism (of a similar inspiration) deserve some treatment because the presently rocketing land prices, triggered off by inflation and the accompanying speculation, are draining considerable funds away from productive investments. These are important contemporary symptoms of a financial disorder. It is also not within the

---

[1] E.g., S.J. Patel: 'World Economy in Transition'. In C.H. Feinstein (ed.): *Socialism, Capitalism and Economic Growth*. Cambridge, 1967.

present scope to review Marx's solution in which the falling profit rate is traced back to the growing organic composition of capital. This relationship is usually derived now as follows: the value of commodities produced yearly, T, is a compound of, or can be broken up into, three parts:

$$T = c + v + s$$

where c is the value of the advanced means of production (intermediate inputs), and $v + s$ is the newly created value—partly paid labor v, and partly unpaid expropriated value s, also called surplus.

The profit rate is the ratio (π) of this surplus to the capital advanced (in this description the combined value of means of production and wages, $c + v$). This means

$$\pi = s/c + v$$

Let us use the Hebrew Aleph[2] for the organic composition of capital, again expressed by the same variables:

$$\aleph = c/v$$

Let us designate the rate of surplus, i.e., the ratio of unpaid to paid labor, with the letter Beth.

$$\beth = s/v$$

Now, dividing the denominator and the numerator by the paid labor v the following is obtained

$$\pi = \beth /(\aleph + 1)$$

It can be seen from this equation that if the rate of surplus is constant (it has proved to be a historically rather stable ratio) then, with the growing organic composition of capital, the profit rate must decrease.

Let us put this train of thought into simple words: since surplus value originates from labor it bears a more or less constant propor-

---

[2] I will revert later to this notation. Let us for the time being accept it simply as a symbol.

tion to wages, and since, with a growing organic composition of capital, wages amount to an ever-decreasing share of the capital advanced, the profit rate must show a tendency to fall.

In reality, however, the interdependence is more complex. Although the above, rather flat, theorem can be read into the Marxian framework, it is, strictly, contrary to the basic thinking of Marx and also to common sense.[3] For the sake of simple analysis, Marx often used the assumption of annual turnover times, although he knew this assumption was only a simplification. As one of the consequences of this simplifying assumption, capital advanced and capital actually used up become identical and cannot be distinguished. Elsewhere, mainly in the second volume of *Capital*, Marx treats the implications of the differences between the two and variations of turnover times in detail and elaborates the view that, in the case of machinery, the capital advanced is usually ten times the capital actually used up in one given year while, in the case of buildings, the turnover times are even longer. As a matter of fact, this idea of simple one-year turnover times which Engels, with all his good intentions, failed to resolve in all the volumes of Marx he edited, has misled Marxists on countless other matters also.[4]

Closer scrutiny shows that the equations derived above imply only that, if the ratio of wages to profits remains unchanged, if the wage cost of production diminishes, the profit rate must also diminish. This is no cardinal rule and does not reveal much about the basic trends of capitalist production. We are interested in the relation of profit to capital advanced and not in the profit margin. Only the

[3] This caused difficulties and there has been no end to attempts to prove the 'Marxian theorem' statistically. See, e.g., Gillman: *The Diminishing Rate of Profit*. Közgazdasági es Jogi Könyvkiadó. Budapest, 1960. The author is quite at a loss in attempting a definition of variable capital and is, therefore, unable to say anything worthwhile about actual trends.

[4] Perhaps it will be enough to mention Morishima (*Marx's Economics*) and Steedman (*Marx after Sraffa*) who, analyzing the famous problem of the transformation of values into production prices, fail to realize that all the rules they state concern only cost prices and not production prices. For this reason their 'rebuttals' and 'theorems' are rather esoteric, holding only in a nonexistent, imaginary economy where all the capital advanced is always fully used up during one production period.

former can show the rate at which the capital advanced may be increased via accumulation of profits.

Profit margins, the relation of profit to costs, may remain constant, increase or decrease without yielding any inference with respect to the movement of the profit rate. Therefore our equation must be set up once again, reckoning with turnover times, that is, clearly distinguishing between stocks and flows, advanced and reimbursed capital.

This is all the more necessary because the formula presented cannot hold scientifically. It is a mismatched formula with a 'dimensional error' in which the equality of the quantities figuring on the two sides is impossible in principle, irrespective of the actual values that they might have. The two sides as set out are, strictly speaking, incommensurable and are not really worthy of being introduced into an equation.

The left side actually displays the rate of profit designated by the Greek lower case letter π. This amounts to a certain percentage *per year*. Its definition clearly requires a period of reference, a certain time unit.

The right side, however, displays a quotient of pure numbers which is without a specific dimension in itself. Both the rate of surplus (a quotient of flows) and the organic composition of capital (a quotient of stocks) represent proportionalities. This is why the Hebrew alphabet was used for these pure numbers as other alphabets have been exhausted. (Greek lower case letters designate turnover times and Latin lower case letters designate flows while Latin upper case letters designate stocks.)

Changing the implicit time unit on the left side from, say, one year to two years or to one month, changes the numerical value of the profit rate because 3 per cent a month and 3 per cent a year do not mean the same thing. But no matter how the time unit is changed (and consequently the numerical expression of the profit rate for the given time unit altered), nothing may change on the right side because the time span is absolutely irrelevant to proportions expressed in those pure numbers. This means that the equation is invalid. Although its interpretation is seemingly sound, its use in mathematical form yields sheer nonsense or, more accurately, points to an omission because it lacks something whereby its two sides would be rendered commensurable.

So, let us start afresh, but this time let us be more careful about definitions.

The profit rate is the relation of surplus value to capital advanced. However, the capital advanced does not consist only of those means of production manifested in the value of annual output, i.e., means used up and wages paid out. These are yearly value flows and not stocks or capital. According to the exact Marxian definition, total advanced capital consists of constant and variable capital. Let us use the symbol C for constant capital (this Latin upper case letter indicating not yearly flows but actually a capital advanced, usually tied up for several years) while V will be the symbol for variable capital. The symbol s and the interpretation of surplus value are unchanged, its essence being really that of yearly value flow, provided that *yearly* profit is considered. Thus the correct relationship will be the following:

$$(1) \qquad \pi = s/C + V$$

So we see already that the earlier formula was mismatched because only a pure number would have expressed the relationship between flows. The present formula is correct because the dimension on both sides is 1/year, as is normal for indicators of turnover times.

The organic composition of capital expresses the relation of constant and variable *capital*, not of value flows. Thus

$$(2) \qquad \aleph = C/V$$

The only correct definition in the earlier discussion was that expressed in the formula for rate of surplus value so it will be used as it stood

$$(3) \qquad \beth = s/v \qquad \text{(that is, } s = v \, \beth\text{)}$$

But we will also need another relationship not stated earlier, one relating variable capital to the yearly wage fund. This is the number of yearly turnovers of the variable capital.[5] Let it be represented here by the Greek letter γ. Thus

(4) $\gamma = v/V$,   (that is, $v = \gamma V$)

We are ready now to derive a correct formula. Considering (4) in equation (3) we obtain $s = V \gamma ב$. Substituting this in equation (1) and then dividing the denominator and numerator by V we obtain, in accordance with the definition of organic composition (2), and arrive at

(5) $\pi = \gamma ב /(א + 1)$

While this formula bears some general resemblance to the previous one, it will be noted that turnover time or, rather, the number of yearly returns of variable capital, not studied earlier, also figures in it.

It can be argued that, if the organic composition of capital increases and if the number of annual turnovers of variable capital remains constant, the profit rate must really decline. But, as a rule, the organic composition of capital increases just because variable capital turns over faster. Thus the impact on the profit rate may be cancelled and, what is more, in some cases (when the number of returns increases faster than the organic composition) the profit rate may even increase.[6]

The main question now is whether or not these quantities and proportions are measurable. The answer is that, although the basic trends can be traced in statistical abstracts (and, at least until the turn of the twentieth century, the trend obtained beautifully), substantiates the Marxian forecast both in respect of the increase of

[5] K. Marx: *Capital*, Vol. III, Chap. 4: 'The impact of returns on the profit rate.' Engels designated the number of annual returns of variable capital by the letter n.

[6] In my book *Cycles and Control* (*op. cit.*) the impact of all the turnover periods on the profit rate is analysed in greater detail. The final result is as follows: if variable capital returns more quickly than constant capital (a rather general feature after the advent of industrialization), the increase of organic composition will, contrary to the general belief, *raise* the rate of profit, even though this upward trend will steadily decelerate. It became practically negligible under present conditions and proportions.

organic composition and a decline of the profit rate. However, by the nature of things, these tendencies were becoming more and more uncertain and they are presently patently unreliable and erratic.

A brief review of the method of measuring variable capital is necessary here to explain this perplexing situation. In the last footnote but one there is a reference to Engels' contribution to the devising of a practical method (variable capital consists of all those wages paid up and recorded as costs of semi-finished and finished products in an enterprise that are not yet sold), which assumes that circulating and variable capital have a common turnover period. This is approximately true in most practical cases.

For the purpose of measurement it is therefore necessary to assume that all components of the working capital—the cost of raw and auxiliary materials, overheads, etc.—will turn over with the same speed. This is generally a fairly good but still not quite accurate approximation. It will not cause any problems as long as the organic composition remains moderate. But with growing organic composition (already in the times of Engels, in the cotton mill used as an example in the year 1871, the value of $\aleph$ was greater than 38, indicating that only 2.5 per cent of the total capital served as variable capital) the ratio C/V cannot be computed without a growing degree of uncertainty.

The problem lies not only in organic composition tending towards infinity but also in the reduction of V to infinitesimal magnitudes. The fall in the variable capital may not halt at zero but may take up small negative values as well. This implies that, around the zero value of V, the index of organic composition switches from plus infinity to minus infinity, i.e., the index makes a jump here. It is a point of discontinuity, and the organic composition behaves most unpredictably around this point.

Is negative variable capital practical? Of course. The baker sells his bread every morning and collects that 'variable capital' which he has actually not yet advanced. He will only pay his workers at the end of the week or the month. In the case of such a baker—and in industries with short production periods in general—the variable capital is actually lent by the workers to the entrepreneur and therefore this variable capital figures as a negative magnitude. Liabilities in the balance sheets of many an enterprise show an item for wage debts of the enterprise, indicating that up to this amount the variable capital has been lent by workers. If this amount is higher than the wage tied up in unsold finished and semi-finished products then the variable capital will be negative and the organic composition will be similarly negative.

For all these reasons, the change in the organic composition of capital was tangible and easy to monitor even on the basis of relatively primitive statistics in times when small-scale commodity production was being replaced by the 'sweat shops' ('Verleger,' a form that may have been only sporadic in some countries) which engaged themselves mainly in supplying staple items and perhaps the needed raw material to craftsmen working at home. At that time it was not necessary to advance any fixed capital and the working capital itself consisted mainly of variable capital. The organic composition started to grow with the switch to manufactures because then all the means of production were already owned by the entrepreneur. With the spread of machines, the share of fixed capital was further increased in industry although (as is shown in Engels' computations) initially the factory buildings were still rented by the entrepreneur. But by the turn of the century all the big factories moved into buildings of their own and, consequently, the share of fixed capital was again surging. By then the share of variable capital began to become negligible and from that time on the above method of analysis turned less and less dependable.

It would not help to improve the statistical service and measure variable capital more accurately, though this task is feasible both theoretically and practically. But as noted above, a discontinuity appears in the index of organic composition at small values of V and in this neighborhood computations become totally unreliable even in case of an otherwise exact measurement.

Marx's theory of the growth of the organic composition has been useful but, most importantly, its correct interpretation reveals its own limitation. After the turn of the century and still more surely since the great depression of the thirties we have reached these very limits. Therefore we have to look for other methods in our quest for explaining the trends of the profit rate and the growth rate. Kalecki acted in the Marxian spirit when focusing on the orders of magnitude of total and fixed capital and its relation to the value of annual production, once measurement of variable capital became so elusive. Doing so he directed our attention from the study of pure proportions to a more thorough analysis of turnover times and mainly to the capital/output ratio.

Growth Scissors

The theories of Smith and Ricardo about the falling rate of profit proved to be mistaken, and Marx's, though correct, has become unsuitable for the purpose of a reliable analysis under present circumstances. Nevertheless, the classical theories most assuredly anticipated that the development of the division of labor is not an unlimited source of economic growth. Speaking more exactly, although a significant and ever-increasing part of economic growth originates from the differentiation and specialization of work,[7] somehow the very same factor retards as well as limits the rate of growth and, consequently, the notorious retardation of growth (and the falling rate of profit) seems to be historically inevitable.

This process can be followed easily by means of the growth model discussed above, and with the help of available data sequences, at least with respect to the stage of industrialization, without requiring an extension of the area already covered by statistics to the field of the reproduction of the workforce, not so far subjected to exact

---

[7] This is what Marx described by the term 'intensive expansion,' as against simple extensive growth, where a given setup of the division of labor is 'blown up': more workers, more factories, more goods. This expansion is obviously limited by the number of workers available for production. Having achieved full or relatively full employment, in the absence of technical development, further growth is impossible and stagnation is unavoidable. Moreover, stagnation must sooner or later turn into a crisis due to the unsold and unrealizable surplus.

assessment. It will be seen that, at the same time, this analysis demands a certain amendment of the model: we have to discard the assumption that the magnitude b of capital intensity and the value $1 - a$ of the saving rate are constant. These changes have already been treated theoretically by Kalecki in his analysis of the acceleration and deceleration of growth.

These values, the 'parameters' of our model, change in a specific and manifest way throughout the process of industrialization in any given country. The values of both a and b do practically and must theoretically exhibit a growth tendency.

Why does b, the value of capital intensity, increase in the course of industrialization? Because labor-saving is an important impulse in industrialization. It is facilitated by a more advanced division of labor, by the use of machines and equipment, and by the enhanced volume of production. However, all the three listed factors of higher productivity induce the growth of capital inputs, both absolutely and relatively, i.e., in relation to the value of the produced goods. For the purpose of a rational division of labor, all phases of processing the object of work must be undertaken in simultaneous and parallel operations, and this in itself increases the necessary stocks of raw materials and 'semis,' that is, the working capital. Moreover, bigger stocks must be held to secure the smooth flow of production along all its phases in order to enable the worker to work continuously; the objects of his work must wait for him and not the other way round. The use of machines thus greatly increases the fixed assets, especially when the transmission system activating the machines gets increasingly sophisticated and indirect. With the growing size and space requirement of machines, industrial production is moved into suitable buildings and halls and most of these have to be matched with similar enormously increasing space requirements for moving and storing the raw and auxiliary materials to be processed, as well as for stock-piling the finished products.

At the same time, urbanization is boosted by the concentration of production: new homes and quarters need to be built and furnished, along with communal and service buildings. Public roads and transport systems need to be organized and these, together with the means and networks of energy, transport and communication, represent the most capital-intensive sectors of the economy. Even though the production of the means of production may be cheapened by higher efficiency, during the fifty to seventy years of industrialization the capital intensity of production increases continuously and significantly. On an average, this growth is about 1–2 per cent per year and sometimes higher, and this means that, at the end of the stage of industrialization, capital intensity is swollen to a multiple of its initial value.

This growth can be shown statistically for every country that underwent or undergoes the stages of industrialization, and it also holds for countries where industrialization is now being started. Moreover, capital intensity appears to grow faster in countries whose industrialization period is historically later than in countries already industrialized. The probable reason is that late-comers to industrialization enjoy the relative advantage of establishing themselves on a foundation of well-known, available and relatively up-to-date technology; they do not have to go pioneering into unbroken or not thoroughly surveyed areas. However, they pay quite a heavy price for this relative advantage because they need to obtain this new technology from abroad. And they have to pay the price established in the international market for machines, equipment and new technologies, though initially they can offer only goods produced at their much poorer level of efficiency. Industrialization thus demands greater efforts and inputs today than in the past, even if it can be accomplished in a shorter time, after which the economy is in the possession of the most advanced technology. There are some countries—like Japan, for example—which have undoubtedly made up for much of their backwardness and even advanced to the top in a number of fields. However, it is not a necessary consequence of unequal development that the late-comer is, automatically, at an advantage: in case of a narrow-minded industrial policy based on obsolete sectors and void of technical foresight, backwardness may persist, even harden.

Parallel with capital intensity, the share of intermediate inputs will also grow in the course of industrialization, although this latter parameter, being a quotient limited by 1, also has its economic limits and so its growth will be less pronounced, seldom exceeding 1 per cent per year. Once again, this is a natural process because the different spheres of production are tied together closer and closer by the developing division of labor: any one product is turned out in more and more phases of operations, more and more branches participate in some way in its creation, more and more hands touch it before its final emergence for use or stock-piling. The share of past labor in the value of the product is thus rising,[8] and this is only another expression for the steady decrease of the share of live or present labor.

The share of intermediate inputs is represented by the parameter a in the aggregated model, but we also have a more detailed description of it, the matrix A of the input coefficients which demonstrates the detailed system of origin and destination of all the goods that ever revolve in the field of production. Input-output balances were drawn up for many countries and for some of them also at different times and it became clear that in less-advanced countries internal relations are also under-developed; there are relatively few elements showing a value other than zero in the corresponding balance sheets, and the table will be slowly filled up only with the advance of development as more and more sectors enter into mutual and direct relations.

This was first reported by H.B. Chenery at one of the first international Input-Output Conferences.[9] His detailed study revealed that only 10–12 per cent of the income of under-developed Asian and African countries originates from manufacturing industry, the bulk being earned in the extracting industries and in agriculture. (As noted earlier, the economy of these countries consists mainly of subsistence farming, that is, very few marketable goods are produced.) In these countries, the manufacturing sector comprises mainly textile and food industries which obtain their raw material

---

[8] See, e.g., Bródy: 'The Share of Past Work in the Value of the Products'. *Statistical Review*, 1958, 1.

[9] The Geneva Conference of 1961.

directly from agriculture. The domestic market for manufactured industrial products amounts to only 5–6 per cent of the intermediate inputs and half or more than half of such products are also imported.

With the advent of industrialization, the demand for the products of manufacturing industry increases about twice as fast as per capita national income. Industrial production begins to proliferate, the home market is expanded and domestic production starts to compete with imports, even if not in the field of new machinery or latest technology, at least with respect to the maintenance and replacement of old machines and other durable means of production.

As a result, the share of intermediate inputs in production, a value not exceeding 25 per cent in the case of India or Peru for the fifties, begins to grow.[10] Finally, the total share of intermediate inputs settles in advanced and industrialized countries at a value of .5–.6 (that is, 50–60 per cent of total costs) and, if wage cost and taxes are added, the resulting percentage will be 88 to 90, leaving an average profit margin of 10 per cent after sales.

The growth of this share undoubtedly slows down with the accomplishment of industrialization and it will eventually begin to stagnate. Professor Carter's study for the United States[11] shows, on the basis of tabulations for the years 1939, 1947, 1958 and 1961, that the final proportions are substantially stable, although the internal structure continued to change.

The dependence of most sectors on the general sectors—namely, services, energy production, information, transport and commerce—gets strengthened. As the economy grows, relatively more coordinating activity is required. However, these growing needs are balanced by cuts in other inputs. The input of materials shows a general decrease. At the same time, the improvement of materials and the improving technology of their use create growing specialization. According to Anne Carter: 'Durable goods are made

---

[10] H.B. Chenery: 'The Use of Inter-industry Analysis in Development Programming'. In T. Barna (ed.): *Structural Interdependence and Economic Development*. Macmillan. London, 1963.

[11] Anne P. Carter: *Structural Change in the American Economy*. Harvard University Press. Cambridge, Mass., 1970.

of lighter and cheaper materials and their designs are more compact...' Demand increasingly shifts towards electric, electronic and measuring instrument industries and tends to decrease for industries fabricating goods from ferrous and non-ferrous metals. Says Carter: 'For a period of alleged technical revolution, structural change seems a bit sluggish.' The change is fairly rapid in a few fields (like labor inputs, the aircraft industry, coal mining and production of measuring instruments), but in other fields it is rather gradual.

We will return later to the problems of the growth of 'mature' countries,[12] but let us first examine the consequence of growing capital intensity and intermediate inputs in the course of industrialization.

If the rate of growth a country can attain is given by the quotient $(1-a)/b$, it follows that, along with the increase of a and b, this rate must slacken in the course of industrialization, and by 2 to 3 per cent a year on the basis of the orders of magnitude quoted above. Initially, industrialization always shows great dynamism and the usual annual growth ranges around 8 per cent. This high rate will necessarily drop to one-third or one-quarter in the course of the 50 to 70 years of industrialization. This is how, finally, the yearly 2–3 per cent growth rate evolves, the slow growth so characteristic of industrialized or 'mature' countries.

However, there is another important facet of this slowdown which is rooted in the fact that the parameters of the growth equation are no longer constant but also undergo changes over time. This forces a specific correction of the growth path: the internal proportions of the economy must be adapted to growing capital intensity.

Changing capital intensity was recognized at an early stage by growth theory and the ICOR (Incremental Capital Output Ratio) index was more and more widely used after the Second World War for the analysis and planning of trends. This ratio expressed the relationship between investments and the consequent increase of production. The unsuspecting reader may believe that ICOR will express the change in capital intensity, that is, it will be a time

[12] Carter (*ibid.*) actually shows signs of falling capital intensity after 1939.

derivate or a logarithmic derivate of capital intensity $b:\dot{b}$ or $\dot{b}/b$. Closer scrutiny reveals the fallacy and also shows that this index is rather unreliable, and 'ill-conditioned' enough to be useless for the purpose of analysis or planning.

The change of investments is expressed by its time derivate $d(b_t x_t)/dt = b_t \dot{x}_t + \dot{b}_t x_t$, if b itself is changing, which is marked by the suffix t. Dividing this by the infinitesimal increment of growth d $(x_t)/dt = \dot{x}_t$ the result obtained is $\text{ICOR} = b + \dot{b}x/\dot{x}$.

The ICOR index is therefore the sum of the time derivative of capital intensity and the average capital intensity, where the former also has to be multiplied by the reciprocal value of the rate of growth $x_t/\dot{x}_t$. However, the growth rate is powerfully fluctuating and its reciprocal may take on practically any value between plus and minus infinity. A near-zero, small increase of production will enormously magnify this index, while a similarly near-zero small decrease of production may result in an extreme negative value. Thus a point of discontinuity is found in this indicator around $\dot{x}_t = 0$. A similar problem was encountered in the analysis of the organic composition of capital and there, too, the decision had to be the omission of the indicator because of this inconvenient feature of the formula.

Changing capital intensity stipulates certain changes in the mathematical model as well. In such cases saving must cover not only the capital requirement of growth but, in addition, also the change in capital intensity. Therefore the new shape of our basic equation will be the following (once again omitting the index t and stressing that b is also variable):

(1) $\qquad (1-a)x = d\,(bx)/dt = d\,(b)/dt^{\dot{x}} + \dot{b}d(x)/dt = \dot{b}x + b\dot{x}$

From this we express the growth rate, i.e., the logarithmic derivate of production:

(2) $\qquad \dot{x}/x = (1-a)/b - \dot{b}/b$

This result is important and interesting from two aspects. First, it pronounces that the rate of growth is no longer constant. Even if the value of $\dot{b}/b$ is constant, or nearly constant, owing to an increase of value b the value of $(1-a)/b$ will continuously decrease.

70

It is still more important to note that the value of the theoretical growth rate, that is $\lambda = (1-a)/b$, is no longer equal to the growth rate of production since this latter rate is less by $\dot{b}/b$. That is, it is practically and numerically 1 or 2 per cent lower than the first 'theoretical' value and this gap is an absolute and not a relative one, a point to be well noted. If the theoretical growth rate is 8 per cent, then production grows by only 6 per cent; if theory yields 4 per cent, then growth is only 2 per cent per year; and if the theoretical rate stands at 2 per cent, then actual production will stagnate. These latter two percentages are actually absorbed by growth in capital intensity and therefore no growth can result from it.

But what purpose is served by a 'theoretical' growth rate once production increases at a much lower rate? Isn't the model deprived of its meaning, exhibiting a growth rate which apparently has nothing to do with the actual course of events, that is, which is significantly higher than real growth in the case of a growing capital intensity?

A closer look at the model shows that this theoretical value is *still* a perfectly practical one as it expresses the rate of growth of fixed capital:

$$
(3) \qquad \frac{d(bx)/dt}{bx} = \frac{\dot{b}x + b\dot{x}}{bx} = \frac{\dot{b}}{b} + \frac{\dot{x}}{x}
$$

Substituting for $\dot{x}/x$ from equation (2) we arrive at

$$
(4) \qquad \frac{d(bx)/dt}{bx} = (1-a)/b
$$

That is, the logarithmic derivate of the growth in capital is equal to the theoretical growth rate given by the model.

In this way, theoretical analysis shows that, in the case of growing capital intensity, i.e., in the course of industrialization, the growth of capital inputs will be typically faster than the growth of production—a characteristic *scissors* develops between the two growth rates in the long run. This scissors can be practically experienced in any industrializing economy, whether it is a planned or market-oriented economy.

71

But this is not the only scissors opening wide in the process of industrialization. A similar growth scissors will be noticed if the growth of savings is analysed, because of the growth of the parameter a.

The growth of savings is actually as follows:

$$\textbf{(5)} \quad \frac{d(1-a)/x/dt}{(1-a)x} = \frac{(1-a)\dot{x}-\dot{a}x}{(1-a)x} = \frac{\dot{x}}{x} - \frac{\dot{a}}{1-a}$$

Expressed verbally this means that savings lag behind the growth of production, again by 1 or 2 per cent a year, owing to the increasing division of labor. Part of the increment of production is again absorbed by the relative growth of intermediate inputs.

The data indicating the orders of magnitude of the scissors may be summarized for the initial period of industrialization as follows:

The amount allocated for investments increases the fastest and its growth rate is in the range of 8 per cent. Total production increases at a slower rate because about 2 per cent per annum is absorbed by the growth of capital intensity. Therefore, the total growth of production cannot surpass about 6 per cent a year.

Still slower is the increase of the national income because part of total production serves the relative growth of intermediate inputs. Therefore, national income cannot show more than about 5 per cent growth.

However, due to growing capital intensity, an ever higher percentage must be invested from this national income. Thereby, part of the increment of income will be absorbed again, and national income available for consumption will not permit more than about 3 per cent growth per annum.

These scissors may become particularly dangerous because the difference in growth rates is absolute. If, owing to the falling rate during industrialization, the growth rate of investments is pressed down to, say, 5 per cent, the increase shown by national production will be only 3 per cent a year, per capita national income will grow only by 2 per cent and, consequently, living standards will necessarily stagnate and occasionally even deteriorate.

It is unnecessary to enlarge on all the economic and political strains caused by these unequal rates; the contemporary world provides ample daily illustrations in industrializing countries. A classical illustration is also available: the first manifestation of the 'industrial revolution' in the history of West European development during the past century. This is the tension which *The Communist Manifesto* described as follows:

> (The worker) becomes an appendage to the machine.... The cost of production of a workman is restricted, almost entirely, to means of subsistence...and for the propagation of his race.... In proportion, therefore, as the repulsiveness of the work increases, the wage decreases. (Moreover); in proportion as the use of machinery and the division of labour increases, in the same proportion the burden of toil also increases.[13]

The picture presented in *Wage Labour* and *Capital* can be summarized as follows:

> The more productive capital increases, the more widespread is the division of labor and the use of machines and equipment. The more widespread is the division of labor and the use of machines and equipment, the more rivalry will prevail among workers and the more their wages will shrink.

This is the strain from which Marxist political thinking drew the (right) inference concerning the relative pauperization of the laboring class and the (wrong) inference concerning its absolute pauperization while, once again wrongly, failing to distinguish the universal problems of industrialization from the specific problems of capitalist production.

[13] Karl Marx & Friedrich Engels: *The Communist Manifesto*. Harmondsworth, 1967, p. 87.

The very same tension is the one which must eventually yield to intensive expansion or, more precisely, a type of intensification in which the indicators of capital intensity and intermediate inputs will not be strained any further. If these indicators do not grow then the growth scissors may snap shut again and the growth of investments, of national product, of national income and standards of living may proceed smoothly and free of tensions.

This kind of 'smooth' growth was characteristic of the advanced, 'mature' industrial states after the Second World War, after the completion of the recovery period, that is, from the late fifties throughout the sixties until the beginning of the seventies. In the next chapter, I will touch upon the background of this relatively smooth growth, rather nostalgically regarded today as the 'golden age'. Here, only one of its features needs to be investigated, the one that resulted in new strains disturbing the smoothness of development and appreciably slowing down the rate of growth from the early seventies.

It was noted that the capital intensity of production began to decrease slowly after reaching a peak in the 1930s. The new technologies then devised saved not only labor but also capital. This 'capital saving' was probably possible because of the expanded volume of production. However, the main market for increased production became defence: first preparation for the Second World War and then for waging the war and, finally, in the aftermath when defence expenditures kept on mounting.[14] Although a reverse opening of the scissors would have been made possible by the decrease of capital intensity in itself, i.e., living standards could have grown at a higher rate than production and investments, this did not happen. The rapid rise of living standards that could,

[14] According to the study by W. Leontief and F. Duchin ('Worldwide Implications of Hypothetical Changes in Military Spending'. Institute for Economic Analysis. New York, 1980) military expenditure amounted to 3 to 14 per cent of the GNP in 1970 and generally showed an upward trend in 1980. The percentage of spending increases with the development level of countries, although there are exceptions: for example, in Japan defence expenditure is extremely low; in China and in all the oil-producing countries, notably high military spending is recorded.

theoretically, have been achieved with the growth and intensification of production was counter-balanced and, indeed, frittered away by growing defence expenditures.

However, at the same time and for this reason, new difficulties and strains accumulated, but this time in areas where they are more difficult to demonstrate for lack of statistical records. The main point is that the rapid growth of living standards, at a more robust rate than that of production and investments, should have been not only possible but would also have met the needs of those decades. To support this statement adequately it is necessary to make a brief detour. Owing to the lack of detailed statistical data it is not yet possible to establish a short and concise numerical proof and we have to fall back on conjectures. As already mentioned, the explanation of the rate of economic growth requires the fullest possible consideration of all the inputs relating to the reproduction of the workforce—current inputs as well as costs and activities tied up for a very long period of time in raising families, schooling, health, etc.

With Janossy it may be argued that the only possible explanation for the relatively fast growth rates observed (which exceed 10 per cent and quite frequently reach 20 per cent) during periods of recovery, is the plentiful availability of trained workers who seek employment. It can be demonstrated that such 'economic miracles' or, more precisely, periods of rapid recovery, last until the available workforce has been totally absorbed by production.[15] In such times, the economy is in a position to make free, or nearly 'free of charge,' use of means accumulated earlier, consisting of human knowledge, know-how, practice, accomplishment, ideas, and also human faculties and opportunities developing and emerging relatively abundantly owing to rapid development.

Janos Kovacs provides a detailed statement of the enormous

---

[15] One has to agree with the remark made by Tibor Erdos (*Közgazdasági Szemle.* 1967. Vol. I, pp. 97–107) that it is extremely difficult to locate the end of a recovery period on the basis of 'reaching' a given trend line, because of the uncertainties of statistical measurement and, let us add, because of the cyclic nature of growth. The cycles actually get started afresh after each period of recovery and the first over-investment is usually caused by the rapid growth rate of the recovery period itself.

amount of these funds previously invested in schooling and professional training as well as the extremely long 'production times' or periods of gestation.[16] However, in spite of agreement with respect to the basic problems, economists have not developed a sound point of view concerning the exact classification of the funds tied up in the reproduction of the workforce nor concerning the classification of the activities that serve human life but are not strictly marketable. Therefore, and also because of the considerable difficulties of measurement, no statistical data or data series are available for the purpose of a reliable analysis of the level of means tied up here and the evolution of this field through the ages. In the first chapter we had to be satisfied with comparisons in terms of mere orders of magnitude. It was stated that wealth amassed in the knowledge of the working force is at least seven times greater than that invested in production and amounts to more than double the tangible national wealth.

Nevertheless, though we are unable to quote exact statistics, the probable movement of this enormous and enormously neglected resource can be easily sized up.

A pioneering researcher into these problems, T.W. Schultz, showed[17] that the number of constant per capita school years[18] of the American population increased *more than six-fold* from 1900 to 1957, and that its growth amounts to eight-and-a-half times if this extraordinary investment is measured not in hours but according to its cost at constant prices.

The following conclusion can be derived from the above: the growth funds tied up in human beings far exceeded the rate of growth of the national income and we cannot go wrong if we estimate it at twice the latter's growth rate. Schultz's investigations also show that this growth became more vigorous after 1929, that is,

---

[16] Janos Kovacs: *A Munkaero Tarsadalmi Ujratermelese es Tervezese.* ('Social Reproduction and Planning of the Workforce'.) Akadémiai Kiadó. Budapest, 1970.

[17] T.W. Schultz: *Investment in Human Capital.* Free Press. New York, 1971. Tables 8.2 and 8.5.

[18] Changes in teaching periods and the general percentage of attendance are also reckoned in constant school years.

after the great crisis, and received a new impetus after the Second World War.[19]

It is, therefore, fairly clear that, while after the thirties physical capital intensity began to decrease somewhat, 'human capital intensity' was growing. Schultz's reading was that total capital intensity may have remained relatively unchanged, but bearing in mind the ever faster growth of fields other than schooling—such as, for example, research, health, other spheres of learning and all the mechanical equipment of households—it is a fair guess that the total capital intensity tended to grow.

Whatever the exact trend, and though we are yet unable to express it numerically, one feature stands out clearly: the structure of the funds tied up changed, and changed rather significantly, in favor of all the means tied up in human beings. Under such conditions and for the material coverage of this process it would have been obviously necessary to have the growth scissors reversed for the benefit of faster rising incomes of workers, that is, of a faster than average improvement in living standards. But this did not happen and therefore the evolving new structure was retarded. The conditions for prospective growth have been gravely undermined by this retardation, as will be shown in the subsequent discussion.

But what are 'the conditions of prospective growth;' indeed, how can we detect the buds of development in the offing, already hidden in daily life; how can we make them flourish? The living conditions and the progress of coming generations depend on whether these seedlings are fostered with care or ignored through indolence. How does 'progress' happen or languish?

Max Planck once comfortingly told a young scientist, perhaps Heisenberg, that new knowledge is not spread by the scientist by his success in persuading his contemporaries but by a growing new generation, already 'accustomed to the new truth'. This anecdote may contain a touch of irony since it shows Planck, then already an

---

[19] Competition with the Soviet Union also played an important role here. The bare numerical comparison of schooling statistics actually caused a big shock in the United States. They were scared that they would fall behind in the field of training and schooling.

elderly man, as still responsive to innovation. Nevertheless, the pronoucement was a very important one and, from the point of view of economic development, even a cardinal one: people enter into the social, economic and public life of their age with an amassed treasure-chest garnered practically in their first twenty or twenty-five years; the character, scope and style of their activities will be basically imprinted in these formative years, even if their knowledge and behavior change and develop somewhat in later life.

In this respect, people differ from machines. The operation and technical standard of a machine is unmistakably determined and set by its year of production. Nor do people resemble animals; animals can absorb only a minimum of training, may be tamed somewhat and taught, but only during a short period of their life-span. Humans do preserve a relative flexibility of mind and body for a much longer period than does any other mammal and the more talented a person the longer will he retain the capacity to absorb new ideas. True, he pays the price in terms of prolonged vulnerability in youth. Yet he does not remain malleable and receptive for all his life-span; his mind and habits become set, and this is just the point so strikingly made by Planck: Humans are not like putty or plasticine; they will not remain soft and pliant for ever. The imprints of their first formative 20–25 years are decisive ones. Let us therefore review the present status of science and education responsible for the instruction and training of these tender minds.

A Scientific Interlude

I spent the first half of my adult years in various industries and held diverse posts, from on-the-job worker up to general manager, both under conditions of planned economy and market economy. In the second half I worked in research and education, again spending about equal spells at universities, institutes and laboratories in the first, second and third worlds.

Recalling the shift between these two kinds of activities I believe the worst shock was caused by a severe cut in salary and, especially, a great loss in personal authority, budget and freedom at the moment of arriving in the sacred field of research and education. Though working hours were set less strictly, this was partly delusion: the worker or the general manager naturally stayed at home with a flu whereas such a trifle was not enough to justify missing your lecture or conference.

Even the holding of scientific degrees and important scientific posts did not entail a broader material and financial freedom. As a skilled worker it was much easier to exert control over my earnings; moreover, the precision machine entrusted to me, together with an almost final authority to decide whether a precious semi-finished part was suitable or not for further processing, represented much greater material value than ever encountered in my scientific career. As a general manager, the sphere of my authority was naturally even wider. Nowhere in scientific life does one enjoy such un-challenged prerogatives.

I do not imply that the scarcity or lack of means was a special impediment in the way of scientific activities. While involved in research projects, the organization of university departments or scientific conferences one does handle fairly large sums. Yet one has to accustom oneself to the fact that even the smallest financial outlays cannot be undertaken without *ex ante* approval or approvals which usually demand more and more lengthy reports, more and more pains-taking back-up and ever-increasing paperwork. According to institute regulations, I am entitled to authorize amounts up to the value of 500 Forints (about $ 20.00) but, as I repeatedly noticed, the teller did not pay without first obtaining the permission of the chief accountant and, thus, here again approval depended on a written preliminary report.

As a skilled worker I simply walked up to the tool-shed for any expensive cutters and others gadgets I needed. Now it requires consi-derable red tape, effort and perseverance to get a few pennies worth of school chalk, stationery or ballpoint pens; of course, to be honest, I have never been denied them. One has to fill forms to get one's work distributed, and in one's capacity as head of a section one may be simultaneously in a position to give clearance to one's own application.

Musing about the distrust and caution, certainly addressed not to my person but to my scientific activities, I discerned a social and an economic reason for them.

The general suspicion is addressed not to the scientist but to his pursuit. The behavior of scientists and scholars is the object of anecdotes everywhere. In the States, for example, they have been nicknamed 'egg-heads' and are considered a deviant element of society, absolutely unable to conform or walk the well-beaten path. And with some justification, because a scholar worth his salt must do his best to discover new roads which are then a nuisance for others.

The economic hand-cuffs are applied to keep a check on his eccentricities. Indeed, you cannot really control a scientist for, if he deserves the name, he must be superior in his own special field, and his peers will be other scientists, perhaps his rivals, and by no means his direct boss. His face will never reveal whether he is actually working or idling, thinking or only guessing what he will get for lunch that day.

The profound suspicion towards the scholar and the feeling of impotence encountered in trying to control him by the normal social means prompts society to subject the scientist and the teacher to assorted obstacles, hurdles, check-points, and other, apparently unnecessary, botherations. It must safeguard its coins as ardently as Moliere's Harpagon did, for the scientist and the research worker clearly intend to waste them since, as all economic theories agree, such people thrive on the workers' toil anyway and are kept by others. They never participate in productive work and, besides, are pretty fresh when it comes to repartee. 'What are you doing now?' a minister once asked Faraday. 'Something you may tax later on,' came the brusque answer, without any hint at electric power generation.

An analysis of this public aversion and its implications shows that the danger lies not, or not primarily, in the comparatively meager rewards and the inferior social status accorded to scientists, research workers and teachers. This is a natural outcome of the trade union movement and wage campaigns in which workers in branches with short production periods are unquestionably at an advantage. Things become intolerable in no time if bakers won't bake, if garbage isn't removed, if transport comes to a halt, or if water or electricity supply is cut. But a 'refusal to work' by teachers and research workers would only have ridiculous consequences. Students would not mind[20] and scientific papers could still be continuously published for quite some time because the backlogs in publication are reckoned in years rather than in months. This way, the salary of research workers and teachers can only fall.

But this is not the worst of the harm done to science. True, the scientist cannot live on air, yet his performance is not closely related to his salary. My lectures delivered at universities in California or Zambia for more dollars or pounds than Hungarian universities and high schools can afford to pay in Forints for the same purpose, were surely not better than my seminars at home—and one does not neglect courses or lectures even if one does not hope to get any remuneration.

From Curie to Pavlov and from Marx to Gramsci, it has been established that the scientist can and does work amidst the worst possible financial distress and even in prison; '...he dreams happy dreams on a bed of nails'.

So the worst problem is not the financial remuneration. But how could Plato have continued to dream his happy dreams being obliged not to lie on a bed of nails, but to present the budget of the research programme for the coming year to the officer of The National Science Foundation, stating details of the planned postal costs and administrative inputs and providing proper justifications in support of the predictable indicator of returns his dreams may earn? Or how could he go on day-dreaming while preparing his annual report to the Hungarian Academy of Sciences, giving proper explanations of how and to what degree his dreams served the resolution 'of the tasks of our government,' how they were coordinated with the general projects approved by Department 9, and presenting in

---

[20] The only success that can be expected is from a strike of those working in kindergartens and teachers of first forms: then there would be no one to look after the children.

suitable detail how far his work fell in the categories of basic research or applied research or development?

Catch 22 works against the contemporary scientist as follows: the office in authority assigns to him the task of directing his scientific field. The office functions according to *old* principles whereas the scientist seeks *new* knowledge or else he is not a scientist. In the resulting clash between old and new, both the office and the scientist are consumed.

All the figures projecting beautiful patterns of growth and stating all the enormous rates at which the different countries increase their spending on research and development that impress the unsuspecting reader as great sacrifices for research and expressions of a glowing love for science are in such circumstances mere indicators of a process in which the Office (or Business) renders Science subservient, according to considerations which it may find appealing but which are usually useless and obsolete at the moment of their birth. The growth of the records of sums of money spent is perfectly compatible with the shrinking time spent on the cultivation of genuine science.

The diluted staff working in science (and education) proper may be one of the reasons why time spent on actual scientific research may remain unchanged or even decrease in spite of increased monetary outlays. As the desirable volume of scientific research and by now, in most cases, the appointment of researchers and teachers are decided either by the Office or by Business, there is now hardly any university in the world enjoying true autonomy as, say, Cambridge once did. There are more and more people who try to perform scholarly and educational functions not as professions, but as occupations. Immense amounts of money are allocated to perfectly unscientific and fruitless research projects on the basis of grandiose promises made by charlatans or by mediocrities having good manners and the right connections. At the same time it may happen that funds required for the continuation of research are denied to Nobel laureates because 'their point is not clear,' or because of their often blunt manners or their 'unacceptable' and 'unintelligible' requests.

Another reason for indifference may be the fact that in the past research seemed to be provided gratis; it did not cost anybody anything and, therefore, no records were kept about its volume although, supposedly, broad circles of the intelligentsia cultivated it. Science was actually carried forward by scientists usually as home work, as a hobby, in their own free time. Therefore the scientist was also free in that capacity. If Mendel decided to sow peas of different colors then that was his own damn business—and if this established genetics, nobody really cared. Einstein, too, elaborated the special theory of relativity not while holding a scientific post at the Kaiser Wilhelm Institute but as a clerk of a licence bureau. By the way, his job and membership in the Academy and the Institute were instantly suspended as soon as he happened to trespass the views, not at all scientific, represented by those offices.

However, the leisure time of scientists and teachers and of the constructive intelligentsia as a whole has rapidly and ominously shrunk during the past century. While wage workers achieved the transition from a working day of twelve to sixteen hours to eight hours and even to a working week of thirty-six to forty-four hours, the working day of the perfectly unorganized intelligentsia has increased from the initial three to four hours a day to eight to ten hours, and in some cases even to twelve to sixteen hours. Sundays have been consumed in the process and holidays have also been practically buried. It is not uncommon for a university or secondary school teacher to have sixteen to twenty-four contract hours a week. Considering that an hour of lecturing costs at least as much, if not more, time in preparation; adding to this time spent in the correction of papers, being on duty, holding consultations, conferences, board meetings and so forth, it is clear that it is no longer possible to maintain the old high quality of performance. Thus the teacher or research worker will not have any leisure time left to him even if he is not forced to undertake a part-time job or a commission as an expert consultant—another growing global symptom.

The spread of part-time jobs is *not* proof of the pragmatism or money-grubbing of this stratum. It is proof of their shoe-string budgets. Where is the professor of the turn of the century with his weekly two hours of college lectures attended by 10 to 20 pupils, who produced two or three talented and worthy successors after the work of a life time, conveying to them his knowledge, soul and heart? Today the contact between the professor and the army of 200 or 300 undergraduates in the first term is through loudspeakers and he does not know much about the habits of his graduates even when they are in their last term.

It may be that this way the cost of science and education is much reduced and, therefore, apparently more economical. But I believe that this is the very point where the roots of the problem may be found. The fact that economists analyse the 'returns' on research or education or that, both in the west and in the east, they try to mould its assessment according to the prevailing standards of investment appraisal, or to assign decisions concerning the financing and location of science and education to planners and economists, is just as strange and hateful as would be leaving the ultimate decision on marriages to expert geneticists.

There is no standard mould suited to science and education, to scientific work and training, because these are not reproductive activities. There is no copying or imitation; what it does or should bring to life never existed before. Productive workers are paid because they create value, products consumed by society, and, therefore, these products have to be continuously reproduced. But science and education do not produce such consumable values; their output is far more lasting. Their work is aimed at understanding, utilizing and changing the conditions of nature, production and society, and if this understanding and change are successful then the output, no matter how minute it may be for a given moment, will attain an infinite value by virtue of its lasting quality. Strictly speaking, it is *incommensurate* compared to productive work in the conventional sense of the term. Ferenc Janossy puts the point most lucidly:

> The productivity of work is increased by research not for a given time but for all time to come. Therefore, if saving achieved on the basis of research is computed as a value, it would give an infinite value.[21]

[21] *The Trend of Economic Development and the Period of Recovery*. Közgazdasági es Jogi Könyvkiadó. Budapest, 1966, p. 137.

It follows that if it is stipulated, as is done in business investment, that the costs relating to research and education should be recovered within a deadline of say 3 to 5 years[22] through the 'consequent savings' or if, before research work is begun at all, an 'explanation' is required which is expected to be clear to all, then the allocations to science and education will quite surely be ungenerous; the interests, methods, procedures and object of science will be *ab ovo* restricted, and real basic research hampered.

This process of the degradation of science to the level of merchandise and all the false expectations attached to it have been manifest since the 1930s and are steadily gaining ground. The implications are extremely dangerous for science itself and the indirect impacts are similarly harmful from the point of view of adequately understanding and *changing* the conditions of production and society, of the processes of adaptation.

Janos Neumann, too, was thinking about this process, about the increasing interference of society and government in the affairs of science, when he morosely remarked, 'Many scientists regret this, and I am one of them.' He elaborated:

In regulating science, it is important to realize that the legislator is touching a matter of extreme delicacy. Strict regulation, and even the threat or the anticipation of strict regulation, is perfectly able to stop the progress of science in the country where it occurs. The fact that strict or unreasonable regulations may deter mature scientists from pursuing their vocation, or from pursuing it with that degree of enthusiasm which is necessary for success, is in itself important, but it is not the most important fact. What is more fundamental is this: The numbers of new talent which accede in any one year to a given field of science are subject to considerable oscillations. They decrease or increase in response to the emergence of new interests, to changing social valuations, to new developments in the field in question, or in neighboring,

---

[22] Janossy emphasized that development does not and cannot produce any kind of 'profit'. Only the *monopoly* of an innovation may yield profit for a while.

scientific or applied fields, etc. I am convinced that seemingly small mistakes in regulating science may affect the reproduction of scientists catastrophically.... Great intellectual values could be lost in this manner,...damage to fundamental science would...cause comparable damage in the technological, and then in the economic sphere.[23]

For all these reasons, Neumann was absolutely convinced that the natural way of functioning of basic research, and especially its two pillars—freedom in selecting subjects of research and freedom in the publication of results—must be maintained and safeguarded.

Well, these are the very freedoms which, together with leisure, are being eroded and lost in all parts of the world in varying degrees. I admit that scientists may be blamed also for the commercialization of science, for its becoming mere merchandise, and for its being subjected to outside control. But what else could they have done once scientific research had grown more and more expensive and free time at their disposal shorter and shorter? As we know from the example of Faust, the scientist will make a deal with the Devil himself to satisfy his curiosity—but, alas, he brings damnation not only to his soul but also to his knowledge.

Let us try a speculative test: assuming that, at a given moment in time, basic research becomes absolutely impossible and ceases and, consequently, the subjects taught at universities get petrified over five or ten years. At what point of time will the impact of this development begin to retard technical changes and the development of production appreciably?

One of the most successful inventions of our times is the Xerox copying machine and different other versions of this technology. Working at the Battelle Laboratory which advanced the first Xerox unit, I learnt that the original publication containing observations about the practical use of photosynthesis (by the way, itself a

---

[23] *Collected Works*. Vol. VI, Pergamon. Oxford, 1963, p. 500. Neumann's susceptibility is easy to understand since he was forced to leave two countries because of the numerous clauses and little mistakes of regulation, i.e., threats of regulation in Hungary in 1926 and Germany in 1931.

product not of basic but rather of already applied research) came to light in the German language in 1905 in an article by a Hungarian author. If basic research had been stopped in 1910, the copying machine would still have not been invented.

Spans of 50 to 100 years from basic research to utilization, from recognition to actual innovation, are not rare. Radioactivity was discovered in 1896, the atomic bomb followed 50 years later, atomic energy plants came about 70 years later, and they still operate in their first, most primitive, costly and dangerous form.

Or let us take the social sciences, say the notion of freedom and equality, which is nearly 200 years old if we accept the French Revolution as its first pregnant manifestation.[24] How far has the world gone in giving reality to these ideas?

Everybody will agree that the physical, natural and technical sciences are far more advanced than the social sciences and this produces an extremely dangerous and unstable state of affairs. Recognizing this menace, Janos Neumann wrote an important treatise under the title 'Can We Survive Technology?'[25] All the same, five or ten times more is spent *all over the world* on the cultivation of the physical sciences than on the social sciences, not to mention the ideological shackles which act as constraints everywhere although in substantially different ways. Adorno gave a perfectly apt description of the contemporary status of the sociologist when he wrote: 'The self-sacrificing work of the scientist consists...in giving up his non-existing ideas against a miserable pay. Today...the scientist is replaced by a better-salaried chief of office...'[26]

Owing to 'apparently little mistakes of control,' inter alia because the findings of the social sciences are less suitable for transformation into merchandise than the findings of the physical sciences, the development of the social sciences has been lagging for a long time. As Keynes wrote: 'Practical men are usually the slaves of some defunct economist.... The ideas which civil servants and politicians

---

[24] If we go back to the Age of Enlightenment, when the ideas were put first on paper, then this span of time is even longer.

[25] *Op. cit.*, pp. 103–4.

[26] *Fact, Value, Ideology*. Gondolat Publisher. Budapest, 1976, pp. 272–3.

and even agitators apply to current events are not likely to be the newest.'[27]

The Enlightenment of the seventeenth and eighteenth centuries prepared the ground for the rapid growth of research and productivity in the nineteenth and twentieth centuries by its respect for intellect, rationalism, research and science. The new tendencies developing in the twentieth century set extremely powerful impediments in the way of the free examination of the primary problems of all the conditions of production and society. And this is the deep flaw which plays so ominous a role in the present-day deceleration of the rate of growth, exactly because its implications have not yet been able to assert themselves in full. It will be practically impossible to prevent its impact being felt for another twenty or thirty years even if, heeding the alarm that has here been sounded, the leisure, liberty and respect enjoyed by scientists, research workers and teachers till the end of the last century is immediately restored to them.

Productivity

The final outcome of research and teaching is improved productivity of labor. We have now to consider the role of productivity in growth, the impact of new knowledge and new technologies on the structure of production and, last but not least, whether there are reasonable grounds to fear that future growth of productivity will be slower than in the past.

In the literature and in planning practice one often finds that the growth of productivity is added to the growth rate indicated by the model because the growth model, at least in its original form, does not show any change in productivity. But this is not justified: the rate given by the model is the rate of the maximum possible growth and nothing can be added to it. Productivity itself is determined in the context of the model and is governed by its inherent proportions.

[27] *General Theory*. Macmillan. London, 1961, pp. 383–4. Note that, in spite of all his originality, Keynes himself was captive to rather old ideas and only his opponent Friedman could top him in resuscitating still deeper strata of conservatism.

There can be no change of productivity without a corresponding change of the structural parameters. (The data of the model allow us to compute both labor productivity and capital productivity. The model also yields respective weights to add those productivities into 'total factor productivity'.)

In handling productivity I formerly departed from the ideas of Janossy who assumed the long-range rate of growth as 'implied' by the proportions of the changing occupational pattern of the workforce.[28] In his opinion, the increase in productivity 'is not a quantity that could be derived from some other factor anyway, since this coefficient is actually the quantitative parameter of economic growth itself, i.e., of a qualitative process.'[29]

I formerly maintained that the growth of labor productivity is a *residuum*. If we subtract the growth rate of the active population (determined by demographic factors) from the rate of equilibrium growth, then the growth of productivity will be the precise remainder. This view is based on the observation that it is equally correct to compute the rate of growth either by considering the purely 'technical' aspects of the production process itself or, if we start from the other side, by considering the growth rate of the active population and the predictable growth rate of its productivity. This is logically sound because, in principle, the same result must be obtained both for growth experience in the past and growth planned for the future.

I later studied mathematical transformations describing the sectoral differences of productivity and an unchanged rate of long-range growth.[30] Despite its mathematical attractiveness, this study was not too fruitful, most probably because the rate of growth itself is strongly influenced by changes in productivity and by a fairly random introduction of technical innovation. Although, logically, this does not militate against maintaining a constant internal structure, its practical value is minimal. If a scientific theory is valid only for a

---

[28] 'The Trend of Economic Development and the Recovery Periods'. *Op. cit.*, p. 262.

[29] *Ibid.*, p. 209.

[30] 'Cycles and Control'. *Op. cit.*, paragraph 3.3.3; and 'The Modelling of Structural Transformation'. *Sigma*, 1979, 2.

special case, the information it can provide is meager and all its beauty and truth are of little avail.

So I returned again to the ideas of Janossy, first of all to the interdependence he revealed (or rather only perceived) as existing between productivity and the occupational structure, and tried to find out what determined this very structure. The answer is obvious: it is knowledge, education and training, human choices, and again, technological possibilities, whereby the main structure of individual occupations unfolds.

Janossy convincingly shows that investment alone cannot accelerate growth if there are no experienced workers and engineers who, let me quote our poet Jozsef Attila, 'know the name of the machine'; he also makes it clear that for the same reason money spent on R & D is not by itself sufficient to promote productivity.

From our own point of view, the essence can be summarized as follows: a perfect harmony must exist among all human activities, ranging from research and education through development and training to investment, and to proportionate production, up to the last little cog—and the same harmonic proportions must prevail with respect to all the 'equipment' needed for all these activities, be it machines and buildings or technologies, or know-how and experience, or knowledge, libraries and the arts.

This is an extremely broad and almost too comprehensive expression of the notion of equilibrium, but it highlights the fact that the general rate of advance will be eventually limited by the field that is relatively lagging behind.

Such a general 'harmony' must be—or, more accurately, ought to be—achieved; *the lagging areas must, therefore be promoted*, even though, sometimes, some of the lagging activities and their 'equipment' may not bear a price tag or, perhaps, any exactly measurable dimension, and even though the desirable proportions keep changing, not rapidly but steadily, over time.

It is admittedly easier to describe this task than to carry it out. It requires two things, each fraught with its special difficulties. First of all, the lagging areas must be identified—and the longer the time span or production period of the process in question the more difficult it is to ascertain its actual lag. Then the proper balance must be restored—and, once again, the task will be the more complicated the longer time it takes from the time the intention is expressed to its actual accomplishment.

When, say, the supply of the output of bakers falls behind the desirable measure it will be noticed in no time and may be rectified soon, provided it was not triggered by lags in other fields with longer production periods, e.g., if flour, ovens and bakers are not available.

The time needed for rectification will be naturally affected by the promptness of trouble signals and by the strength of the motivation and the vigor of the action taken to redress the balance. Differences in the amounts of time required for rectification may be caused by the relative roles played by market mechanisms and by planned control.[31] But whatever the difference, they are both powerless against those time lags that determine the physical process. Bakers' ware is perishable and only a few days production can be stored; its period of production is of a similar magnitude and, therefore, shortage or over-supply noticed on one day can be corrected on the next.

The control of products with longer production periods and longer life-spans is a more delicate issue. Housing is a clear example. The life-span of apartments is normally 40 to 120 years and the building of new ones is a rather slow process with long gestation periods. The available supply and type of apartments is, therefore, rather rigid. Considering that in this field equilibrium cannot be reached from one day to the next and not even from one year to the next, a lasting shortage of certain types coupled with over-supply of certain other types is frequent even in countries with vigorous market motivation.

Still greater are the difficulties of control at the fountainheads of productivity: in research, education and training. Here problems

---

[31] Planned or *bureaucratic* control is predominant even in the running of American supermarkets or bread factories. It would be absolutely impossible to run them by motivating each baker, salesman and clerk according to 'profit maximization'. However, this bureaucracy is extremely refined and is based on data processing by fast computers.

caused by the extremely long gestation periods and persistent good or bad conditions are topped by the difficult and frequently laborious assessment and measurement procedures resulting from the fact that the 'output' itself is not amenable to easy definition. How are we at all able to notice any imbalance with respect to new knowledge required for innovation in production or with respect to its application? How can we identify any lag or dysfunction in such areas?

The very substantial difficulty of assessing failure in this sector and in even understanding the problem is best appreciated by assuming a situation of maximal dysfunction, in which all sources of innovation have been depleted for good, and there will be no more new machines, no new products, no new technologies, no new knowledge or inventions. However, those facing such a situation will not immediately become aware of it. Let us take, for example, the engineering industries in a situation in which the list of machines available has frozen and also their capacities, technical parameters and productiveness. The lack of really new models has never been an obstacle to describing and advertising the old models as brand new. Both market and planned economies emphasize 'the new' and take hardly any notice even if the 'new' thing is actually the same as the old one or the change is not substantial.

According to our assumption, educational curricula have ossified. The same lectures are read, the same slogans are repeated, the same textbooks are published and the same subjects are taught in the same way at all institutions of higher, secondary and primary education. Teachers may well be almost happy about this because the continuously amended textbooks and changing teaching schedules were a nuisance anyway. From now on, students will keep marching out, two abreast, with strictly uniform and stable knowledge.

All this in combination would, of course, be disastrous. Even the steady growth in the numbers of scientific papers, periodicals and books (shown by statistics to have doubled at an unbroken pace every twelve to fourteen years since 1750) would slow down. General productivity would still grow: that of machines is capable of increasing *suo moto* for about another twenty years and that of labor for another forty years. In spite of the sudden and sclerotic calcification of the scientific arteries, the actual efficiency of production will increase in practice through the replacement of old machines and old people by new ones—until the productivity of every machine reaches today's maximum, until knowledge becomes absolutely universal, again at the highest standards prevalent today. Considering that this process of replacement, this change from obsolete to less obsolete, may last for decades, measurement will not be sensitive enough to reveal a slight slackening in the growth of productivity and will not yield any sign of the profound disaster that has already struck.

It is like looking at a cold, extinct star through the telescope: the star has ceased to exist but its rays keep traveling to us across the enormous distance.

Why is this doomsday fog so thick? What blurs our vision? We are unable to measure productivity itself—productivity does not possess any absolute level—nor do we measure changes in it; we measure only the change of *average* productivity. This average is the mean of the old and the new and with the decay of the old this average will keep rising, because the old dies even if the new remains unborn.

How wide is the difference between loss of productivity and awareness of it in a given population? Janossy demonstrates this through a striking example:

When an old worker retires at the age of 60 he passes the baton to his grandson just beginning his active life. His son, the father of his grandson, still works. However, the relation between the respective levels of productivity of the three generations must be the same as in the series Italy, England and the United States, where productivity approximately doubles with each step. If somebody begins to work today, he must produce four times more than his grandfather did otherwise the 3.5 per cent annual growth in productivity cannot be maintained. In industrializing countries where, through the transfer of more advanced technology, the growth of productivity may reach 6 per cent a year, the son will produce 11 times as much as his grandfather, and he must surpass even the *average* productivity of his own times by two and a half times or the yearly 6 per cent growth will be *impossible*.[32]

The difficulty of interpretation is due to taking (wrongly) the average to be a numerical value equally applicable to everything or everybody, although in reality the average is formed from extremes. There may be a ten-fold, nay, a hundred-fold difference between the productivities in different countries, and during the process of industrialization a country will multiply its original per capita production ten or a hundred times. Similarly, the factories, workshops and workers in any country are scattered over very broad intervals on the scale of productivity. A 1 to 10 proportion is no exaggeration at all of the extent of the actual range.

If this train of thought is carried further and we ponder on how knowledge, now possessed by the new generation, is actually dated, a still deeper insight is gained.

Research findings become subject matters in universities only after a lag of several years, especially nowadays when research and education are artificially separated everywhere. Subjects taught at universities filter down to high and upper secondary schools after further time lags. From there teachers carry them to primary schools and it is another eight or ten years before school-going children learn the new knowledge and implement it in practice.

Therefore the time path considered necessary for the organization of schooling systems in backward countries—a delay which may be as long as the span of one or several generations—remains valid even for the most advanced countries if we consider how long it takes a given pulse of new knowledge to be propagated right through the system.

Of course, it may happen that some partial findings take a short cut or a new technology may directly jump to the factory from the research institute or the university, or factories may themselves run research institutes and educate their workers. This does, indeed,

[32] *Op. cit.*, pp. 240–1.

happen if there is adequate motivation. But let us also consider the other contingency wherein propagation is retarded by simple human forgetfulness. How many of us are able to solve our old exam questions or pass the university entrance examination again at the age of 50? I think only a few of us—and I am not one of them.

As an illustration of the extreme slowness of propagation take the most quickly 'updated' subjects: the sciences, first of all physics and mathematics. In the latter two subjects nearly nothing is taught in primary schools that was not discovered before this century and as for the epoch-making and profound theory of Einstein, high schools do not yet teach it regularly.

So if we speak about the productivity of human labor and about its growth, if we try to measure and assess its level and rate, we must be always aware of the incredibly broad and deep range across which the development of human activities is summed up. This is the reason why increase in productivity is one of the most stable of indicators, showing the greatest degree of inertia over the long run. It is stable enough even to make Janossy inclined to consider it a physical 'constant'. (This high degree of stability, or the tendency to change only very slowly may be compatible with marked cyclical fluctuation.)

In view of this, it is all the more alarming that the general indicators of productivity have, since the early 1970s, increasingly lost their momentum. Of course there are many reasons, both lasting and provisional, for this. The changing prices resulting from the increasingly monopolistic tendencies of the former colonies, and difficulties of adaptation accompanying this are undoubtedly provisional causes. (The problem is not of crude oil alone. It is clear that the terms of trade with the third world have and are going to change with respect to a number of raw and basic materials.) The effects of the characteristic shift taking place partly in the pattern of economic sectors and partly in the age pattern of the laboring class is likely to be more lasting. Here the point is the increasing predominance of services, or of 'general inputs,' to use A. Carter's term. In the United States, 62 per cent of the workers are already employed by service industries. In addition to the low per capita output in this

95

sector, its productivity also grows at a very slow rate and, apparently, there are no expectations of basic innovations which will change this situation.

The second cause of the loss of momentum in productivity is that increasingly younger and, consequently, less experienced generations, are being employed. This displacement could be in favor of enhanced productivity provided the younger age group joins production with higher knowledge, but this does not seem to be the case. That is, at this point, the reduced educational 'reserves' of productivity are already apparent; training does not seem to make headway and, in most countries, it is not paying for companies to invest in the direct education of their workforce because of the high degree of turnover.

The changing age structure of the population—a world-wide phenomenon—is attributed to a host of other symptoms which will be treated in detail in the next chapter. Here it will only be noted that this change in age-structure undoubtedly worsens the prospects for increasing productivity.

The most alarming of all the symptoms is the relative scarcity of innovations, of new technologies and products. It is not just that extremely high interest rates all over the world stand in the way of updating production equipment. For example, the American automobile industry has been only too aware, during the last ten years at least, that it could compete with growing Japanese and German imports only if it manufactured smaller and more economical cars. Yet, in spite of this knowledge, it is both financially and intellectually unable to transform its obsolete capacities of production and, consequently, is in need of ever increasing government assistance (be it in the form of loans, subsidies or protectionist economic measures).

The high interest rate itself is not only a cause but also an effect of the 'intellectual depletion' of technology—one of the reasons why financial capital flees from industry and services into fields of bigger profits: property development, housing and speculation. It is this flight, together with the climbing public debt and inflation, that keeps the interest rate high.

The intellectual and educational reserves of technical development are being exhausted and, in my opinion, the process has been going on for a long time and will continue for a fairly long time to come. This had already become clear to A. Carter in the course of his analysis of postwar structural transformations which he found to be far less significant than earlier structural changes in the light of the new technologies elaborated during the war, strident propaganda and great expectations. Since the sixties, even this slower structural transformation has kept losing speed and has come to be increasingly limited to control processes and microelectronics.

We have, therefore, to survey the field where the intellectual seeds of new technical knowledge and inventions germinate, because at present this seems to be the area lagging far behind the others.

It is very difficult to assess a lead or lag in research and education, the benefits in relation to costs or the trends of these returns, because the impact is spread over a very long time-span, ranging from decades, and often, to centuries. It is somewhat easier to judge whether it is advisable—strictly economically speaking—for a young person to devote himself or herself to a career as a researcher or teacher. Consequently, we are also able to estimate changes in the attractiveness of these fields during the past century.

Janos Neumann was quoted above to the effect that any strain on or control over research (and, let us add, education) will not only mar the enthusiasm of mature researchers who have already become scientists, but will also affect the quantity and quality of new generations of scientists.

A review of relevant data—costs, salaries and time inputs—convincingly shows that, for a long time and at a growing pace, a deep-seated disproportion has emerged all over the world.

In vain are the soothing words of the fellows of the school of 'Human Capital'[33] claiming that investment in university education is more profitable than in high school education and these latter investments are again more profitable than those in primary educa-

[33] See, for instance, G.S. Becker: *Human Capital*. Columbia University Press. New York, 1964.

tion. Comparing costs with the higher remunerations a higher degree can earn, they reckon returns at slightly over 10 per cent. But costs are *ab ovo* drastically under-estimated in this curious 'investment appraisal': it is assumed that students engage themselves in earning money during all their free time and that their expenses are only supposed to cover tutoring and equipment (disregarding the usually high boarding costs in colleges). On the return side, the possible income is then substantially over-estimated because of the inclusion of the 'free' intellectual careers of physicians and lawyers whose study periods are much longer and whose earnings are much higher. The need to subtract incomes originating from property—which are relatively high in the register of university graduates not because they are graduates but, contrarywise, because children from the wealthy strata usually go to university—is forgotten. Yet the picture is not rosy even if the data are accepted at their face value. The sociological sense of the school of Human Capital does not operate and the smooth and serviceable 'discounted present value' computations render them blind to the actual situation.

The real problem may be stated as follows: a qualified teacher or research worker will be able to earn a regular salary only at the age of 22, that is, at least eight years after his classmate, an unskilled worker, became gainfully employed. During these eight years he must spend at least four years' pay on living and study expenses. This twelve-year pay (of which eight is pay foregone and four years pay is actual expenses) will require another twelve years to be compensated if the costs are calculated without any interest and if the salary earned is double the worker's wage from the first moment of taking up work, which is rare in research and simply impossible in teaching jobs. So, by the time his total accumulated earnings reach those of his classmate's, who may be still an unskilled worker, he will be 34 to 40 years old and will have reached the last years of the normal age of reproduction. Perhaps he will be compensated for his difficulties in maintaining a family, for the anxieties he suffers in case he has children, indeed, for all the distress he experiences, by the undoubtedly higher standard of living he enjoys in his last twenty to twenty-six years. But it is hardly reasonable to expect a fourteen-year old student (or his family) to undertake a venture which *might* begin to pay off only twenty years *later*. I do not know of any sound enterprise that would seriously consider an investment with a pay-off period longer than ten years, especially as the salary differentials that *may* be attained in the remote future are known to have been strongly decreasing since the beginning of this century.[34]

An analysis made in the United States showed,[35] for example, that engineers, suffering to approximately the same extent as university professors, lost over 30 per cent of their standard of living relative to the average applicable to workers between 1929 and 1954, and about 40 per cent relative to physicians and dentists. So the latter preserved their salary differentials, their employers not being big companies and governmental agencies. A similar tendency has been observed since the turn of the century, but the lost position is rather naively attributed to the 'excessive offer' of engineers. Still, all this is not considered dangerous because, quoting Friedman and Kuznets,[36] it is claimed that the salary differentials add up to more than the costs of university training. Thereby the scientific degree has been degraded into merchandise like a bond or a washing machine: one buys it if it is worth its price.

A similarly ominous tendency was reported by the Association of Scientific Workers in England in the early 1950s:[37] the scientific

[34] The wise 'Human Capitalists' are also guilty of the little mistake of computing not on the basis of expected salary differentials but with those valid at the time of the decision. This is a mistake which would not seem funny to the board of directors of a company. The perpetrator would run the risk of being sacked on the spot. According to computations by Janos Kovacs (*op. cit.*, p. 128) an average-engineer/average-worker salary ratio above the factor 3 secures smooth reproduction. Before the 1930s this was the case both in Hungary and in most advanced countries but by now it has dwindled below 2.

[35] Blank-Stigler: 'The Demand and Supply of Scientific Personnel.' National Bureau of Economic Research. New York, 1957.

[36] Research was strongly affected by the narrow-minded research work done by Milton Friedman and Simon Kuznets in the NBER, published in 1945 under the title, 'Income of Independent Professional Practice'.

[37] 'The Economic Position of the Scientific Worker'. A.Sc.W., London (probably 1950). On the implementation of the Beveridge plan, it was necessary to adjust the salaries of doctors by statute. The salary of the professors in medicine was thus automatically raised, triggering extraordinary tensions in the field of education and research. The paper argues that the differentials ought to be levelled, but that did not happen.

worker, whose pay had been raised much less than that of manual workers, did not benefit by the growth in production even if it was partly or wholly due to his effort or inventiveness. It was stated that, since 1938, the salaries of scientific workers increased by only 40–50 per cent whereas the cost of living stood at least 90 per cent higher and all the signs showed that this trend would persist.

Indeed, this trend did persist and continues to persist all over the world, although not everywhere to the same degree; but everywhere at least half of the relative living standards of research workers and teachers has been lost since the turn of the century.

A Hungarian analysis of teachers' salaries is also available.[38] Let us consider the salaries of the best paid stratum: the municipal secondary school teachers. Their salaries were 800 to 2000 Crowns in 1876, 1200 to 2380 Crowns in 1896, and 2400 to 5600 Crowns in 1911. This shows that the approximately quadruple increase of prices was not compensated for adequately and thus nearly 50 per cent of the standard of living of teachers was lost by 1911. By 1938 another nearly 40 per cent fall was recorded: 'At present the salary of teachers in the capital...still does not amount to more than 65–70 per cent of peace-time salaries. If peace-time and present prices are considered...salaries are a still smaller percentage of pre-war salaries'.[39]

The inter-war 'peace-timer' was in for another surprise after the Second World War. The 1938 salary of secondary school teachers had been 200–586 Pengo a year. The stabilization of the year 1946 generously granted a *factor 1*[40] to teachers' salaries and so the salary stated on 1 August 1946 was 258 to 435 Forints; in the countryside this was naturally still less, around 204 to 381 Forints.[41] This salary, staggering behind the unimpressively growing standard of living of

[38] Gyula Dausz: 'Szekesfovarosi Oktatok Fizetesugye'. ('The Salary of Teachers in the Capital—1873–1933'). FANSZ, Budapest.

[39] Dausz: *ibid*. The last peaceful year was in 1911 and Dausz used the exchange rate of one Golden Crown to one Pengo.

[40] The factor of workers' wages was above 1.5 and that of staple goods over 3. For more details see Sandor Ausch: *Az 1945–46. Evi Inflacio es Stabilizacio* ('Inflation of 1945–46 and Stabilization'). Kossuth Publisher. Budapest, 1958.

[41] 'A Pedagogusok Berezese' ('Salaries in the Teaching Occupation'). Library of the Trade Union of Pedagogues. Budapest, 1968.

workers, reached the level of 1004 to 1352 Forints by 1 July 1954. (Typically, the salary ceiling increased only 3.1 times while the minimum level had to be increased 3.9 times owing to rising prices. Thus in a career spanning thirty-five to forty years, an especially diligent, devoted and loyal teacher could obtain a salary increase of as much as a 352 Forints, or 35 per cent.) These salaries were not included in the general adjustment in 1957 and although they rose somewhat in 1959, from that time teachers' salaries were placed definitely and clearly below those earned not only by skilled workers but also by better trained semi-skilled workers. Oh, my country! You surpass the advanced West in wasting the best human minds.

It can safely be asserted that the career of researcher and teacher is no longer remunerative. If it is still chosen, it is owing to status considerations (weakening because the social standing of these professions is also rapidly falling everywhere), family traditions (surprisingly, these seem to be gaining vigor), and two features that may have only a hair's-breadth between them: either the student feels that he is predestined to enter research or teaching or that he is not good for anything else. In view of this, it is equally safe to assume that these professions are getting simultaneously narrowed and diluted: a diminishing team of devoted partisans with extra-ordinary talents and selflessness, often bordering on self-denial, float on a sea of ignorance and semi-knowledge consisting of a mercenary army of make-believe research workers and teachers. This army cannot be trusted to have the old efficiency and the consequences of this have been felt for a long time—and will be felt for a long time to come even if standards of social appreciation are transformed tomorrow, which is hardly likely.

Various countries, after undergoing a lot of trouble, crises and losses, and after the lapse of many years, may come to be convinced of the need to change all this. Sooner or later, it will become clear that those countries will do relatively better in which the worth of the teacher and research worker are acknowledged in terms of both social and financial standing, as in the Federal Republic of Germany and Japan, and perhaps in the Scandinavian countries and Canada. The cases of Britain and India are dubious, although there such vocations are, comparatively, fairly well tolerated. America, presented by Hitler with the greatest and most talented stratum of research workers and teachers of all times, has practically used up this resource without managing to establish adequate replacements. 'Why bother when we can buy the best of the world any time?'

The political-minded reader, keen on cherishing his economic optimism, could say: 'No need to ring the alarm bells, no need to cry wolf; a one or two per cent fall in the rate of growth of productivity is not everything; things will recover and flourish again and, at worst, things will go on a bit slower.' However, mankind has not experienced such a robust change in the growth rate of productivity during the past two hundred years, not even in periods when there was good reason to expect an acceleration in the rate of growth.

Schumpeter explained economic cycles (which will be discussed at greater length in the next chapter) as follows: increases in productivity (the technical renewal of the production processes) occur, mostly abruptly, at the end of the economic cycle, inducing a new upswing. His ideas were adopted by Kaldor who formulated an exact theory of economic cycles which was in perfect agreement with observed facts (though, for the sake of logical completeness, it is necessary to explain why innovations occur in clusters). As stated, the theory was in beautiful agreement with empirical facts: the major periods of improvement, the extensive replacement of productive equipment and the updating of technologies always took place around the trough in the cycle. Every economic time series served as a ready illustration of the theory: a falling rate of production was always cancelled by an unusually high growth of productivity; while, in the ascending part of the cycle, at the time of fast growth, the main resources were provided by the powerful increase in employment and the fuller utilization of capacities.

At present, and probably for the first time in economic history, statistics indicate a declining growth rate which is not accompanied by any improvement in productivity, which does not involve comprehensive innovation, but is accompanied by a slackening of growth and a simultaneous slackening of productivity.[42] This is an extremely

[42] This is general enough to support a new theory of Kaldor's, the reverse of his former one: production and productivity go hand in hand.

sinister sign indicating that the intellectual reserves, new knowledge and new opportunities that could bring about a rational renovation of production are depleted. I do not hold that these reserves have run out for good, that the number of new technological licenses does not increase, that there are no innovations, even important ones, in one field of production or another. There are some, but clearly not enough to keep up the customary rate of growth in productivity. And if it is understood that the evolution of this indicator is so enormously inert, if we are aware of the enormous breadth of the range it expresses, then it will be realized that the declining rate is a sign of profound dislocations that have occurred in the fundamentals of the process.

Perhaps it is not *only* the quality and the results of research and educational work that are found to be lacking and not *only* the selection, motivation, remuneration and public appreciation of research workers and teachers that matters—but that they do matter is certain. If we fail to rectify the current state of affairs, the efficiency of the economic process will not develop at the old rate and might even fall into stagnation. Even if we immediately restore the harmonic proportions and the old, or at least a reasonably high, level of appreciation of (and expectation from) these activities, it will still take a long time to halt the downward trend of productivity and eventually to reverse it because these are slow processes with extremely prolonged gestation periods.

Perhaps it is not yet the twelfth hour, perhaps the deterioration is not irrevocable. But let us stop blaming 'objective' factors to justify the slowdown and all the 'limits to growth' as the Club of Rome does. The list of excuses quoted to explain the slowdown includes the scarcity of raw materials, the exhaustion of energy sources and the contamination of the environment—as if it is not we who contaminate it, exhaust it, or waste it, as if we had no reasons whatsoever to look for those factors that are upsetting the necessary harmony. If we keep blaming the small dimensions of the globe, its finite resources, and everything other than ourselves, the best scenario we can expect will require us to repeat our classes.

3

About Cycles

One of our basic assumptions, the equality of savings and investments, was rendered less and less defensible in the course of our discussion. In Chapter 1, it became clear that this equality requires countless further equalities to be preserved and that, therefore, the proportions of production, consumption and growth have to be extremely rigorously maintained. It also became clear that the required proportions and equalities needed to be enforced also with respect to countless activities of another kind which are not marketed and, consequently, are not controlled by the market. The market, as such, can, at best, exert an indirect influence on them. Our assumption concerning the prevalence of such a universal and comprehensive equilibrium thus lost much of its probability and reality. Nevertheless, it remained a fairly obvious theoretical postulate, a very important point concerning the necessary preconditions for a smooth growth path.

In Chapter 2, the idea was further disturbed by new features: it turned out that the proportions that should, in principle, be secured for the sake of a smooth growth are themselves variable. Moreover, the most important proportions whereby the rate of growth is ultimately determined, or at least dominated, have till now escaped closer scrutiny and their measurement is fraught with special difficulties. It is, therefore, extremely difficult to include them in the usual economic accounts and thus also extremely difficult to assess their state of equilibrium or lack of it.

The basic equation has to be faced again and the notion of equilibrium from which the equation was derived needs to be re-examined. By slightly extending the equation and assuming that violation or lack of equilibrium triggers a certain corrective behavior—and we are going to show that this corrective mechanism is essentially the same both in market and in planned economies; and that, moreover, it must be the same in any ecological environment—we come across a special form of motion. This motion is the *economic cycle* rooted in the simple fact that the economy is *never in equilibrium*. Yet, want of equilibrium, in the broader sense, induces a movement *around equilibrium* by way of a continuous adjustment process. In essence, it is this process that keeps the system working: continuous production and even growth is rendered possible by dint of a cyclic motion.

A theoretical analysis of the length of cycles reveals that specific time spans pertain to each activity. The only acceptable method of predicting the expected growth paths of present-day economies is to determine all the wave-lengths of the major cycles and to analyse the superposition of these cycles upon the growth path.

The Equilibrium

Ever since Adam Smith unravelled how the 'Invisible Hand' of the market works, how it guides selfish interests towards a social harmony and how the lack of equilibrium creates a tendency toward equilibrium, armies of economists returned over and over again to the governing idea to examine, analyse and apply it.

Alas, too many things were mingled and have remained entangled in the basic discovery. From the exclusive point of view of our present subject, Adam Smith combined in the same exposition the various ideas that economic equilibrium *exists*, is *optimal*, is *pursued*, and is *achieved*.[1]

However, in the more than 200 years that have elapsed since he wrote, the Harmony he presaged was lamentably lost. I will only question Adam Smith's last statement. With due respect I will try to show that it is neither right nor wrong. More precisely, the 'achievement' of equilibrium is a process that does not move toward equilibrium, but neither can it leave its vicinity. The economy is thus capable of functioning but only with miserable inefficiency.

More daring people contest more of his statements. Janos Kornai[2] distinguished himself by taking a profoundly antithetical position and I have, therefore, to explain why I do not follow him.

In Kornai's opinion, equilibrium 'is not a good thing'. 'The marriage between an impotent man and a frigid woman may be considered as some kind of an "equilibrium" but it can hardly be considered the ideal form of relationship between the two sexes.'[3] Kornai believes that the 'buyers' market,' the general excess of supply, is 'good'. In his opinion it is desirable that 'the aspirations of both sellers and buyers should be intensive and that a type of disequilibrium, namely pressure, should assert itself at this high degree of intensity.' Although in Chapter 22.9 Kornai expressly permits the interpretation of 'pressure' as excess supply, it will yet be convenient to examine the terminology used by Kornai.

I disagree with Kornai in his emphasis on 'a high degree of intensity'. As he holds in his treatise, the intensity of aspiration is hinged on the intensity of economic motivation. If one may judge by historical experience, emphatic motivation (big profits or monetary gains, or obsession with money-making) has caused more trouble than benefit. Taking an analogy from the field of pharmacology (a field where stimulus and response, that is, the question of proper

---

[1] The categories of interest and social harmony will not be considered and other pointers in his sociologically, psychologically and politically fertile thesis will be similarly ignored in this paper.

[2] *Anti-Equilibrium*. Közgazdasági és Jogi Könyvkiadó. Budapest, 1971.

[3] *Ibid.*, p. 309.

dosage, has long been subjected to exact scientific research), it will be appreciated that the minimum of effective motivation still seems to be reasonable and humane. But this observation takes us to moral questions not to be considered here.

However, by imposing a permanent disequilibrium, a constant excess supply, gives rise to awkward symptoms as a result of the 'desirable pressure'. If we persist with it for long it might totally disable the economy. If, following the example given by Kornai, a factory persistently manufactures a million pairs of shoes each year though only 800,000 can be sold,[4] one wonders what will happen to the 2 million pairs of unsold and old-fashioned shoes accumulated over ten years.

Kornai himself perceived the basic inconsistency of his proposition and was, therefore, driven even deeper into contradiction and had to contest the very notion of equilibrium. Here his argument runs as follows: the notion of equilibrium exists but only in models and theories used to describe the economy. However, in reality *because of the lack of conceptual clarification, "supply" and "demand"* are not measurable. Therefore their quantitative relationship (their equality, "equilibrium," difference) does not lend itself to inter-pretation.'[5]

It would be only too simple to confront Kornai here with his later writings and current scientific work in which he returns to the same ideas.[6] At present he uses models giving precise definitions of and measurement to both demand and supply regulated to reach the very same equilibrium path of which he formerly denied the existence. However, the argument touches a deeper problem which is too important to be evaded, whether Kornai shuts his eyes to it or not.

The point is whether there exists in reality anything corresponding to the notion of equilibrium. (This notion, by the way, has an indisputably approximative character and is consequently inaccurate and possibly also unsuited to a clear-cut definition.) In other words, if one defines equilibrium and expresses it in a mathematical model,

---

[4] *Ibid.*, p. 304.
[5] Emphasis in original. *Ibid.*, p. 239.
[6] *The Shortage*. Közgazdasági és Jogi Könyvkiadó. Budapest, 1980. *Non-price Control* (with Martos Bela). Közgazdasági és Jogi Könyvkiadó. Budapest, 1981.

or if one illustrates it in a virtual numerical example (as Marx did) or in an actual statistical tabulation (as Leontief did), does this equilibrium mean anything that may be *achieved* in practice? Does it really *exist*?

Kornai, and along with him the growing ranks of anti-equilibrists, are guided in abrogating the notion by the fact that this equilibrium has never been observed in practice. Why this is so will be explained later. However, this is not enough ground to contest its theoretical and practical possibility. If we contest it, we abandon the most important, nay the *only*, tool that brings some semblance of order into our haunted science. This is why Kornai was forced to return to the field he declared nonexistent.

It is certainly true that an exact equilibrium will never be observed. But lack of equilibrium is a symptom that can be beautifully observed and described. If unsaleable stocks are amassed or if there is a shortage of certain items, if some goods are manufactured at a loss and require state subsidies while, say, electronics yields more profit than the fiscal authorities are able to skim, if the pace of production gains or loses speed, then plenty of very real pointers will be available to show that the equilibrium of production is 'upset'. But this term itself is again misleading: an equilibrium can only be 'upset' provided it existed previously, and one never reads about its existence, only about attempts to 'restore' it. This reminds me of the balance of the rope-dancer. The man is literally never at 'rest' because he has to compensate for the displacement from his pretty unstable state of equilibrium. But this is no reason to deny his equilibrium, to dispute the possibility of rope-dancing or to dismiss the idea of equilibrium as thoroughly uninteresting for the rope-dancer.

So the question to which we seek an answer is: What *keeps* the economy operating *around* its equilibrium state, noticing that it *never is in equilibrium*?

But if it is *not* in equilibrium it will not be valid to claim that our basic equation, anchored to the equality of savings and investment, is correct. On the contrary, we must set out from an inequality, i.e.,

$$(1-a)\, x \neq b\dot{x}$$

Why is it correct to assume lack of equilibrium? Because, in spite of a general and precise equilibrium for almost every product and activity, a single tiny disequilibrium may disequilibrate all the other markets and activities. The division of labor renders the production of every product mutually interdependent and interacting and so disequilibrium will be propagated. But we can go still farther. It may be assumed that the exchange of products and activities is perfectly smooth and equilibrium is total, except for one price being mismatched. However, equilibrium will be again disturbed, the prices of all the other products and services will be displaced from equilibrium and, in the case of a market economy, the volumes supplied and demanded will deviate from the postulated equilibrium.

Let us go further and assume that both quantities and prices are in perfect equilibrium, except for a little lack of foresight: managers anticipate a 5.1 per cent growth instead of an actual, say, 5 per cent. This tiny act of over-confidence, is practically impossible to discover since it is certainly below the usual tolerance of statistical measurement; this covert but, in principle, possible mistake is sufficient to produce excess demand in the market for means of production and to trigger price increases of varying extent, according to the changing degree of excess demand, and so to dislodge the whole economic system from its postulated state of equilibrium.

The equilibrium of an economic system is thus extremely fragile; it requires a treble equilibrium of production, prices and anticipated growth rate. Even the slightest anomaly—more or less rain than usual, late delivery by a partner, a cloudy afternoon leading to lights being switched on in some flats—is sufficient to upset it.

It was thought for a long time that the instruments of planning are much more effective than the market for mastering the intricate and discordant inter-relations of an economy. In fact, a thesis was propounded claiming that a plan secures smooth and steady economic growth. And, indeed, planning was highly successful in some fields. It could really invigorate those activities it found to be particularly important. However, owing to this very fact, it was less functional than the market from the point of view of smoothness and steadiness; it did and does produce bigger jolts and tangibly worse disequilibria.

It has now been realized that in this respect planning has definite limits. Even if the only objective of the plans is to achieve equilibrium and not to maximize growth in some particular fields, the degree of precision and details available to planners would not be adequate to achieve this equilibrium in practice.

Present methods are rather inadequate and it is impossible to reduce the tolerance of statistical measurement to zero. Current inputs are measured within an error margin of 1–2 per cent. For stocks, the uncertainty is still greater and the error may be as high as 10 to 20 per cent. Consequently, the accuracy of planning cannot be much refined. Considering that we have not yet covered the bulk of social activities, neither statistically nor in the plans, and our restricted ability to assess those parts that have been analyzed (the most minute statistical coverage never extends over more than 4–500 sectors), it is clear that planning, too will never be able to secure perfect equilibrium.

Even supposing that, armed with an enormous computer and statistics of extraordinary detail and accuracy, or by operating a congenial economic automatism whose efficiency is far superior to the present market control, the economy can be brought into the miraculous state of complete equilibrium, I dare say that saving and investment will still not be equal!

Both saving and investment take time. Savings must have been accumulated and taken shape before becoming available for investment. Likewise, it is evident that a decision concerning the setting up of a factory will not instantly produce a functioning unit as its buildings need to be designed, its foundations laid, its workshops built up, its equipment manufactured and installed, raw materials procured and production on the new machines test run.

All this needs a gestation period of months, perhaps years, depending on the nature of the productive process in which the investment is made. Such, although usually much shorter, lag periods accompany any increase in production, even if it is accomplished with already existing equipment and under familiar circumstances. These production periods should not be ignored and the gestation period of investment is such a production period: the time required to instal and complete new productive capacities.

Considering these periods of production and gestation one will also note that a product finished today is destined for use only after a shorter or longer period of time. If production grows, current saving must be substantially higher than current investment because current saving serves future investment. If current saving is just equal to current investment, the economy cannot grow and, under such circumstances, it either stagnates or its growth rate slackens.

But if saving and investment are not equal, how should one interpret national income statistics which show equality? Can one depend on such statistics?

The problem is similar as in the case of a motion picture composed of a series of stationary pictures. If the series of stationary pictures is 'dense' enough, the consecutive projection of the pictures, each sharp in itself, will approximate a smooth motion. But if the consecutive shots concern not a given moment but long intervals then the contours of the moving object will be unavoidably blurred. This blur is typical of statistics drawn up for longer (quarterly or annual) periods.

There is still another factor obscuring the picture: certain economic actions can be judged only *ex post*. Suppose in a given year, stocks have increased; this is, apparently, 'saving' because the goods have been produced and they have not yet been consumed in the next phase of the given process. But is it certain that all this is also *bona fide* investment? It may be, provided the increase of stocks proves to be reasonable and future growth in the volume of production justifies *ex post* the past stock-piling. On the other hand, it may turn out that these stocks accumulated simply because they were produced as a result of a misjudgement, in an expectation of a future growth which did not materialize, and the stocks are found to be now unwanted. Such cases do not qualify as investment; furthermore they constitute a burden for the manufacturer whose storage costs are now unnecessarily increased.

Or, say, the foundations of a factory have been laid and the concrete basement of the workshops has been finished. Are all these inputs definitely investment? They may be and again they may not. If the project is going to be completed, the factory will go into production perhaps four or five years later and these outlays may qualify as investment. But it may also happen that, owing to changes in economic, political or technical circumstances, the factory has to be relocated or its technology redesigned, or it may have to be abandoned altogether. In this case, several years later, the entry originally audited as investment will turn into partial or total loss. I have never seen national income accounts in which corrections are made for such losses, which occur regularly but concern past years.

Statistics are again caught in a typical act of default: they presume that the proportions of production are balanced in any given year—something that never happens. Therefore, they chalk up economic mistakes, unnecessary stock-piling, and 'investments' in never-to-be-finished projects which have to be written off later. Thus statistics necessarily show a higher national income than its *ex post* value. The just excuse, however, is that statistics cannot do otherwise: whether all the expectations about saving and investment come true or not is a matter that will only be settled in the future, often in the remote future. This is why none of the practising economists were able to foretell the crisis of the 1930s. Frantic investment and saving created a superficial impression that everything was fine and it was realized only after several years that it was a mistake to accumulate stocks and to launch grand projects which nobody really needed. The ensuing loss was phenomenal.

The hypothetical events discussed above are all closely correlated with what is going to be explained in more detail hereunder, namely, that the major and even decisive inner proportions of economic growth, equilibrium or its lack, even the degree of dislocation, do not lend themselves to direct observation. It is only possible to derive retrospective conclusions concerning the violation of equilibrium or of proportions gone astray. If it is reasonable to suspect that equilibrium may be missed most of the time then a model showing a perfect balance cannot be expected to yield any information about the real course of the economy. Inequality must be *ab ovo* assumed, and the model must be so constructed as to yield a good illustration of the very inequality of investments and savings.

For the sake of clearer interpretation and convenience, let us therefore transform our former inequality to state the discrepancy of saving and investment:

$$(1\text{-}a)\ x \neq b\dot{x}$$

Dividing both sides by the value of total accumulated stocks, bx, we obtain

$$(1 - a)/b \neq \dot{x}/x$$

In this form the equation only states that the theoretical equilibrium growth rate $(1 - a)/b$ is not equal to the actual growth rate observed, $\dot{x}/x$.

The theoretical growth rate was designated by the Greek letter lambda, i.e., $(1 - a)/b = \lambda$. Let us now denote the observed growth rate of the economy, by the lower case letter s, that is, $\dot{x}/x = s$. Now the above inequality can be written simply as

$$\lambda \neq s$$

As was already mentioned, it is strictly speaking not possible to observe either the value of λ nor that of s directly. This is the most irritating aspect of economics in general: these primary quantities are not visible.

It is possible to approximate the theoretical growth rate relying on statistical tabulations but this was seen to be of poor accuracy and also delayed by two or three years, according to the availability of statistical data. The case of the actual growth rate is less cumbersome: it may be computed statistically, but again with some delay and only as an approximation because of the inaccuracies in measurement.

So here we have two growth rates, a theoretical and a practical one. As a rule they are not equal because there is no equilibrium, but we are unable to see or touch or state their difference directly. However, the outcome of their difference and especially of their lasting and durable divergence is a tangible and directly observable phenomenon which always triggers corrective action. In the next section we will see how this correction takes place and what special form of economic motion results.

The Real Movement

How must prices and production move if they are never in equilibrium? Let us take the simplest case first: simple production, the market for one single commodity, the special case from which Adam Smith drew his brilliant inference. According to his argument, in case of excess demand the price increases. A higher price triggers a greater supply and at the same time curbs demand, therefore equilibrium will be soon restored.

However, a hidden flaw in this argument prevented his followers from grasping the real movement of the market. It is of course true that the price is, as a rule, increased by excess demand. However, it needs time for the increase in price to assert itself and become an effectively high price. What was concealed and left unspoken was the time element in this chain of cause and effect.

The real movement is as follows. Let us assume that at the beginning of the process the price stood in equilibrium and only began to rise due to an excess demand. True, the excess demand will be trimmed by the increasing price, but this also needs time and so the price keeps increasing until the excess demand has been completely eliminated. So, after a certain time has elapsed, the original excess demand will have disappeared. At this point of time, demand and supply are in equilibrium, but the price has continuously increased till that point and therefore the present price cannot be in equilibrium because it must stand now above its original level.

Therefore, a reverse process will start: the high price still stimulates supply and further restricts demand. This way an excess supply develops. Of course, as soon as an excess supply emerges, it will exert a downward pressure on the price. Nevertheless, this process similarly needs time and the excess supply increases until the price returns to its original state.

Although the price has now returned to its state of equilibrium, the previous excess demand is now replaced by an excess supply. Thereby the second half of the cycle is launched: excess supply decreases the price, this in turn reduces excess supply but by the time quantitative equilibrium is reached the price rests below its equilibrium position and thereby triggers a new wave of excess demand. By the time the price has been raised back to its equilibrium level by the excess demand we arrive at the end of the cycle, a perfect copy of the state of affairs where the cycle began: with price in equilibrium and an excess demand.

This history is plotted in Figure 2, showing how the price and the quantity fluctuate around their theoretical equilibrium value. In the state of equilibrium, demand and supply are equal; there is neither excess demand nor excess supply.[7] Similarly there is no difference here between prices and costs, the latter including the established usual profit. A high price indicates an extraordinary profit, while a low price entails loss, with their corresponding implications for the suppliers. At the same time, prices influence consumers in the opposite direction.

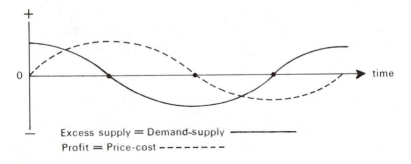

Figure 2
The Movement on the Market

---

[7] Considering Kornai's protests, this could be simply regarded to be the equality of production and of purchases, thereby eliminating the notion of 'demand' and 'supply' which, according to him, are impossible to measure or interpret.

So the economic cycle manifests itself as a natural form of movement already in the simplest of cases. In the case of a growing economy and considering several inter-related activities the picture will be far more complex but the simple model put forward in the previous chapters renders it possible to follow these complications with comparatively simple mathematics.

Mathematical means are absolutely necessary for the explanation of cycles developing in the case of expanded production because the simple verbal explanation is inadequate. It has been, for example, claimed that an excess supply may develop because, previously, prices have been increasing and therefore manufacturing became extremely profitable, that is, more profitable than in the case of the other products that were not considered. But if all the products are equally considered then a general increase of prices does not entail a rise in the rate of profits. If the price of each product increases at a uniform rate, then their costs of production must increase at the same rate. Therefore, the profit rate cannot increase, even though the inputs appear to be of a higher value than previously, because at the same time stocks or capital become apparently more valuable or at least more expensive.

It is also claimed that prices are depressed by excess supply and this is perfectly logical as long as only one product is considered. Yet if this excess supply is general, if each and every product is produced in a proportionately greater quantity than its equilibrium volume, then the economy is obviously back in its state of equilibrium, of course at a higher level. Therefore, a general excess of supply or 'general over-production' is logically an inconsistent proposition.

To all this logical perplexity another very important symptom must be added which the theory of cycles has to explain. The movement illustrated above, with prices and quantities reaching their respective maxima after a certain time lag, can be observed only in very simple markets. Here, first, the price attains its maximum and this, after the lapse of a quarter of a cycle, induces the maximum of production. The movement of production justifies the movement of prices and the movement of prices justifies the movement of production. This yields a logically closed and satisfactory picture, a clear description and at the same time a clear explanation of the cycle.

However, expanded reproduction or economic growth has been found to exhibit a different kind of cycle. In this case the increase and decrease of prices and of production are typically simultaneous. (Since inflation has become the order of the day it can only be claimed that prices rise generally faster in prosperity than during the recession—currently a fall in prices has become a rarity even at times of crises because of the heavy rate of inflation.) Here all reasoning seems to have lost logical support: if prices and production move in unison then they cannot explain each other; simultaneity apparently precludes explanation by interaction.

And so the verbal theories of economic cycles have also failed. They could give good reasons for a displacement from the state of equilibrium. They also described how this displacement generates a self-aggravating process: recession triggers a still worse recession while prosperity 'feeds' prosperity. But this does not say more than the old maxim: 'Nothing succeeds like success.' Nevertheless, the climax (where prosperity is replaced by recession and where it *must* turn into recession) or the trough (where recession turns into prosperity) has never been caught *in flagranti* by anybody and never been described in convincing and logical terms. Either bare descriptions were given or external factors, 'ceilings' and 'floors' were introduced from where production is 'thrown back'. Verbal theories ought to give an immanent and logical explanation of the cycle.

Let us take the path of pure mathematical analysis trusting that the mathematical form will yield a clue to the specific movement of production and hoping that the economic 'translation' of the mathematical result will be suitable for developing a logical interpretation which can also be illustrated with real data. What we want to gain is not only knowledge of the form of this motion, not only its qualitative result and explanation, but also some quantitative information about the length of the cycles.

Let us look at the inequality derived in the previous section and consider its implications. What corrective action will be taken by the economy if disequilibrium emerges?

In the course of economic growth, the demand for any one

product can be split into two parts: the first is proportional to the level of production and the second to the envisaged rate of growth. This second part is particularly apt to fluctuate. If say, a 4 per cent growth is planned instead of 2 per cent, then the demand for investment goods must be doubled while the intermediate demand will only increase 1.04-fold instead of the previous 1.02 (i.e., a relative difference of less than 2 per cent). If now a higher growth rate is planned than the permitted maximum, the result will be an excess demand for all the inputs needed for investment. This excess demand will be spread over a rather broad range of commodities because growth requires not only plant and equipment but also an increase in the stock of raw and auxiliary materials. This is what may be called a general excess demand, even if it does not actually affect literally every product and service.

Of course the 'permissible' or equilibrium growth rate is not exactly known in practice. We have an idea about its magnitude but it cannot be specified accurately. We only know there exists a certain 'theoretical' equilibrium growth rate, denoted by λ. If s, the actual growth rate, is higher than λ there will be an excess demand and if it is less there will be an excess supply. This excess demand or supply may well remain concealed for quite a long time because its initial manifestations are only over-ambitious plans and unusually big orders or, contrariwise, a deliberate slowdown of production and procrastination on usual orders or reluctant haggling.

It may be then that the market responds to this excess demand or supply and indicates their presence by rising or falling prices. But cases are known even in the sphere of market regulation where this response is missing or sluggish because the market is not 'perfect' and the process is retarded by various 'market flaws,' such as, state interference, price regulation, and monopolies. A response must nevertheless develop also in this case, and it will develop also in a planned economy, even a most rigorous form of it, ruled through central directives (although in such an economy prices do not transmit the movement of demand and supply any more and, on the other hand, changes in prices have very little or no impact on decisions concerning production).

However, this excess demand or supply—or, to put it still more simply, the difference between production and purchases—has an outcome which will occur in every type of economy in case of a lasting disequilibrium. Stocks will sooner or later be depleted if demand is excessive or a glut will develop if supply is excessive. These symptoms are open to direct observation and will necessarily force corrective action.

So, mathematically speaking, the thing that affects decisions about production is not the difference between λ and s but its time integral (the consequences of the difference accumulated over time). This will then trigger some economic decisions.

But what is a production decision? I believe I have now come to the point where I must break most sharply with the usual approach of mathematical economics. In my opinion, mathematical economists have failed to discover what is directly manipulated by a 'production decision,' what is the 'decision variable' whose value can be determined. Both mathematical and verbal economic science have shown laxity in clearing up what the managers of the economy may and may not *decide*: the volume of production or the growth of production—or perhaps something else.

Observing planned economies in practise aroused my suspicion that the actual decision very often does not even touch the variable which it aims to influence. For example, we had precise plans about the tons of coal to be extracted or the number of passengers to be carried or the amount of electric power to be generated. But, quite obviously, the plans could not 'decide' these quantities because actual production, actual transport and actual kilowatt-hours inevitably turned out to be at variance with their planned value. It follows that these are not decisions but merely wishes, forecasts or directives.

The plans also detailed the national income to be distributed in a certain proportion between consumption and accumulation so that accumulation and investment should secure a given rate of growth. This was similarly proven not to be a decision variable: proportions evolved at variance with plans and, in practical economic life, it was impossible to fix responsibility for, say, exceeding the planned volume of investment or failing to achieve the planned standard of living.

However, there are decision variables, both at the level of the national economy and of the company. Here real decisions are made and in such a way that the decision has an immediate consequence which takes shape precisely in accordance with the decision. Such decisions are the *starting* of a job lot, the heating up of a furnace, the signing of a contract, the launching of an investment project and so on.

Therefore, in terms of mathematics, the decision variable is neither x nor $s = \dot{x}/x$ but $\dot{s}$. What is decided is the speeding up or the slowing down of the growth rate. With respect to investment this decision means that you can accelerate (i.e., start more than the usual number of projects) or you can apply a brake by starting fewer than the usual number or developing less expensive projects or by spending less on projects under way.

Obviously, by taking these real decisions, whether to accelerate or decelerate, we do influence the speed of growth of production and, ultimately also the level of production. But fully determining an outcome of something and indirectly influencing it are two very different things. Apple production cannot be fully determined in advance, nor is it possible to determine its growth rate. But one can plant or fell apple trees, fertilize them, spray them, water them and so forth—these are real decisions ultimately influencing both apple production and its growth. However, having made the decision, one is at the mercy of reality because the processes one hopes to influence are affected by the decision in a peculiar manner.

This peculiar influence can be grasped clearly only through mathematics as mathematics alone can handle relationships between variable quantities and their differential quotients. The equation illustrating the impact of a decision does not formulate any kind of 'equilibrium,' but expresses the response of the economy, never in equilibrium, to a decision variable: the acceleration or deceleration of the speed of production:

(1) $\qquad \int \lambda - s \, dt = D\dot{s}$

The interpretation of this equation is simple and straightforward. It indicates that the available resources, rich or scarce, measured by the integral on the left side, force an acceleration or a deceleration. For the time being let us take the parameter D as a dimensional constant, securing qualitative homogeneity between the right side and the left side of the equation. At the same time it may be regarded as a factor of proportionality showing just what amount of new investment may be started from a unit of reserves. We will revert to a discussion of its meaning when the solution of the above integro-differential equation has cleared.

Luckily, the equation is one of the simpler ones and, as it is shown by substitution, it is solved by the following function

$$(2) \qquad s_t = \lambda + \mu \cos D^{-\frac{1}{2}} t$$

The function $\dot{x}/x = s$, that is the rate of growth, will be thus a variable fluctuating around a mean value λ with an amplitude μ and a cycle time of $T = 2 \pi D^{\frac{1}{2}}$. It follows that production, x itself, will be a fluctuating function growing at the average rate λ, its exact mathematical form being

$$(3) \qquad x = x_o \exp (\lambda t + \mu D^{\frac{1}{2}} \sin D^{-\frac{1}{2}} t)$$

Here the basic form of the economic movement is obtained. It consists of an exponential growth (a trend) and a superimposed cyclic modulation.

As far as the quantitative characteristics of this form are concerned, the magnitude of the rate of growth has been already discussed, the value of maximum displacement from equilibrium is given by the amplitude μ, while the frequence $D^{-\frac{1}{2}}$ is the number of fluctuations during the time interval chosen as a unit for measurement.

The value of the dimensional or proportionality constant D can now be determined by simple economic considerations. If the intention is the acceleration of growth, the initiation of new investments, the more capital-intensive the investment desired, the bigger the reserves required and the longer these will be tied up outside the sphere of production during its period of gestation. So, if the symbol

b is again used to denote capital intensity and the symbol g for the length of the gestation period then

(4) $D = bg$

From this the length of the economic cycle follows

(5) $T = 2 \pi \sqrt{bg}$

Provided that our theory and the derived form of motion is correct, the following may be inferred as our main corollary:

The length of the economic cycle is proportional to the square root of capital intensity and the gestation period.

With this the mathematical deduction is concluded. The remaining task is a more detailed qualitative and quantitative analysis of the derived form. This will be taken up in the next section.

The only question yet to be asked here is: Does the cyclic movement derived in pure mathematical terms provide any key to an exact and logically sound explanation of economic fluctuations and, in particular, how can it justify the necessary occurrence of turning points in economic movement?

I believe that an essential insight is needed to clear this matter. There are certain not yet considered reserves needed by the economy, some surplus tied up in the process of production (stocks of semi-finished and unfinished commodities as well as initiated but not yet completed investments) the magnitude of which depends not on the level of production nor on the growth rate of production but is decisively determined by the *acceleration* or *deceleration* of the growth of production. These reserves undergo violent fluctuations during the cycle because acceleration or deceleration is a vigorously fluctuating variable, but this violent fluctuation has remained quite concealed till now.

Let us consider the order of magnitude of these fluctuations during the cycle. Production only increases by 20 to 25 per cent during the usual four or five years of an economic cycle. Taking, say, a 5 per cent average growth as a reference point, the growth rate itself already shows a much stronger fluctuation. On the average, over the past two centuries it was found to range from about minus 5 to plus 15 per cent. That is, the growth rate fluctuates much more powerfully than production. In attempting to compare the usual fluctuation of acceleration and deceleration with the rate of growth, the logarithmic differential of s is formed, that is, the value of $\dot{s}/s$ is examined. It is seen to take on every value from plus infinity to minus infinity in the course of the cycle. No greater fluctuation is possible. However, the implications of this value have not been followed up so far. It has not been measured, computed, or attributed any importance. Yet it has been shown above that this value governs the growth process of the economy and is the final decision variable.

It can be statistically demonstrated that semi-finished production and unfinished investments are exposed to extremely strong fluctuation owing to the acceleration or deceleration of the growth process. The funds normally needed to absorb these extremely strong fluctuations are secured by the usual credit operations.

Now we are in the position to present the pattern of the cycle as we did for a single commodity at the beginning of this section. However, the variables now trace different economic categories. Instead of supply and demand we have saving and investment. The price of the commodity is replaced by the rate of interest.

And so the pattern of the cycle can be constructed in the manner of a simple market movement: if saving is in excess of investment then the rate of interest must decrease, because the supply of money capital is proportional to saving while its demand is proportional to investment. If, contrariwise, investment is in excess of saving then, for similar reasons, the interest rate must increase. As before, a 'high price,' that is, a high rate of interest, encourages saving and discourages investment whereas a 'low price,' that is, a low rate of interest, depresses the propensity to save and boosts the propensity to invest.

Western monetary theory derives the miraculous regulatory power of the interest rate from this, and with the same reverence that Adam Smith used to pay to the Invisible Hand. This gave rise to theories on how a desirable equilibrium of production may be created by influencing the rate of interest. However, as was emphasized at the beginning of this chapter, the truth is somewhat more complex. These processes of regulation take time and their form, in principle, is not a convergence towards but a permanent motion around equilibrium.

Suppose that at the beginning of the process the economy is in equilibrium, that investment and saving is about equal but the interest rate is lower than usual. Thereby investment is encouraged and saving curbed; this will in turn react upon the interest rate and will sooner or later cause its increase. By the time the interest rate reaches its equilibrium level the growth of the economy has been strongly accelerated and investments are far in excess of savings. Therefore, the interest rate cannot rest in its state of equilibrium but has to overshoot it. Now investment will be curbed and saving encouraged which is only a polite phrase for the turning-point: after prosperity the economy is thrown into a recession. By the time the interest rate returns to its normal level, savings will be far in excess of investment, so the rate must sink even further and after a while we reach the lower turning point of the cycle.

This provides the missing link in the previous chapter where the Schumpeter-Kaldor theory of the cycle was mentioned. This is really the turning point where a concentrated renewal of the productive equipment becomes due. The entrepreneur must improve and innovate and the banker has already accumulated the necessary savings and looks for oppurtunities to lend them profitably. According to this, however, the cluster of innovations is not a cause but a result of the cyclical movement.

The general course of the cycle is again plotted in Figure 2; only its continuous line has to be interpreted as excess investment (or excess saving), while the dotted line represents the movement of the interest rate.[8]

In this way the market pattern of the cycle is described. It is logically closed and evident but it nevertheless gives rise to certain illusions and, in this respect, it shares the fate of the Invisible Hand, referred to at the beginning of the first section of this chapter.

The specific interdependence of supply, demand and prices deludes us into believing that, through a shrewd manipulation of supply or prices, or perhaps both, economic fluctuations could be

---

[8] Naturally not the nominal rate of interest but its real rate.

prevented. This is the basic assumption of a planned economy: a belief that it is possible to secure a smooth and steady growth by eliminating or taming or manipulating the market.

Similarly, the specific interdependence of saving, investment and interest deludes us into believing that, through a shrewd manipulation of savings or the rate of interest, the quantity of money or investments, cycles of production could be prevented. This is the usual assumption of western economists. Its different facets and prescriptions were developed by Keynes, Friedman and their respective schools.

However, as we must suspect by now, economic fluctuations have much deeper, almost tangible, physical roots. The cycles displayed by prices, supply, demand, interest, saving, investment, etc., are only superficial symptoms; they are not the final reason for the profound instability of production, surfacing from a great depth with overwhelming force. Production, all activity, even life itself, is cyclical...and they cannot be otherwise. The next section, which digresses into imaginary systems, will take up these deeper questions.

An Ecological Interlude

Growth, fraught with cycles, is empirically found to be typical of both market and planned economies. But are we right in not distinguishing these two systems of production when discussing cycles? Are the forms and laws of their economic motion really common? I believe this is not wrong from the point of view of the symptoms under study. If maximizing of profit is accepted to be the driving force of market economies then the maximizing of growth is characteristic of planned economies. This does not imply that there are no other motives in both systems interfering with economic decisions, and these motives may be substantially different. However, maximizing of profit or of growth respectively remains the dominating motive and it is evident that rate of profit and rate of growth are simply alternate expressions for the *same* intrinsic economic relationship. The strict mathematical deduction of the identity of these two rates was pioneered by J. Neumann, although their identity and numerical equivalence had been noted already by Marx.

The real economic objective is specified in the same way, whether we stress the production of values or the creation of use values. Use value and value in exchange is only a theoretical distinction drawn within one single real process which is split into a duality in our minds. An object without a use value has no value in exchange and though the reverse could be imagined (something without a value in exchange may possess use value, therefore use value is a broader category) there is no evidence so far of such use values being taken into consideration by planned economies. Moreover, if there is any historical difference at all, it is that, till now, the planned economies have more strictly limited the range of products and services they consider than do market economies.

If there is no essential difference with respect to the goal, there is similarly no difference in the principal procedures of control. The plan, both in its traditional 'balance' method and in its mathematized versions,[9] forecasts markets, predicts production and consumption (that is, supply and demand) for different products and classes of products. In other words, it simulates future markets. It may be that it overcomes some minor fluctuations in the process of planning computations, but it has been found that it simultaneously ignores certain obstacles and creates difficulties that the market solves relatively easily and automatically. However, on the whole, the plan computation is subordinated to the numerical interdependencies of demand and supply and if the latter induce cycles then these cycles will certainly be imbedded also in the plans, in spite of the best intentions and efforts of the planners. This is not because balance sheets are not kept in equilibrium but simply because of the attempt to keep them in equilibrium.

Setting out from the other side, it will be similarly evident that, with respect to their essential function, the market forces are basically identical to the decision procedures of the planner. As has already been shown by spelling out the equation of motion, the planner can

[9] The Leontief approach or the theory of Linear Programming.

do no more than accelerate or decelerate the rate of economic growth, initiate more or less new investment, and speed up or slow down current investment in accordance with the funds available. The market is similarly not able to do more than inform the agents of production of the situation by indicating the abundance or scarcity of demand and supply, of savings and investments. It is a practically immaterial circumstance that this information is conveyed by the movement of prices and the rate of interest because the decision it prompts in the agents of production is the same as that taken by the planners under similar circumstances.

In this argument it is naturally assumed that both the market and planning economies function, according to their notions, perfectly. But each has its specific flaws. These imperfections may be different and therefore the movement of the two economies may differ with respect to smaller details. The market is mindless: this is both a disadvantage and an advantage because, on the one hand, it is unable to forget anything (a planner may forget about, say, the wooden crates needed for the apple harvest) but, on the other hand, it is unable to comprehend some things (the planner may recognize that higher rents do not necessarily result in more apartments).

Yet all this only concerns details and not the basic motion considered here which must be essentially the same under both systems and has been actually found to be identical.

Now let me take another step and conjecture that their motion must be identical because these two systems of production share the same form of motion with all the other existing or fictive systems of production known hitherto. Let us take an extremely simple ecological system: a flock of zebras grazing in a meadow. The quality and quantity of grass is naturally an external condition. (Such external conditions belong to the growth of every system and if we wish to consider also the internal conditions pertaining to the zebra we may consider the regularity of grazing, the speed of wandering, the average bite, etc., to be such internal variables of adaptation.) This condition determines, irrespective of the zebras' consciousness or intention, whether the flock will increase and at what rate, or whether it will only stagnate or is doomed to extinction.

However, the adaptation to the given amount of grass is a specific process. An over-populated flock over-grazes, thereby restricting its own future increase. Hungry zebras will generate less offspring or, if their numbers stay constant, the young will be weak. The birth and/or survival rates will decrease and probably also the average life expectancy. This way a downtrend is started and once it begins it will go on through one or more generation of zebras. Consequently, the meadow will cease to be over-grazed and will after a while turn succulent again and so a smaller population of now well-fed zebras will once more tend to proliferate.

Fishermen and hunters have for long experienced the cyclical tendency in a number of diverse species. Vico Volterra, an excellent mathematician, gave a brilliant mathematical explanation as early as 1931 in his seminal book, *Theorie Mathematique de la Lutte pour la Vie*. (The equations used in our text are greatly simplified versions of his pioneering ones.)

Is it possible to apply the relationship derived for the length of the cycle also to ecological systems? I believe that an approximation *is* possible in view of the considerations discussed below.

The biological interpretation of the gestation period is evident: it is the time of gestation of the offspring, the usual term of pregnancy. But how can one translate capital intensity? Already in economic systems capital intensity may be approximated through the predictable life-span of the required inputs. This is evident, because every product, once produced, represents a certain amount of value, and this value is tied up in the product till the end of its 'life-span'. The fixed capital of any given country is equal to all the products already produced but not yet consumed. This is exactly how statisticians take account of it. Therefore, the expected life-span in years represents capital intensity fairly adequately.[10]

Let us calculate an ecologic cycle with g as the period of pregnancy and b as the average life-span. We have no data for the zebra but the

[10] Strictly speaking, capital intensity is identical with expected life-span only in the case of simple reproduction. However, this indentity may be extended to the case of expanded reproduction if the expected life-span is assumed to be a probability variable with an exponential density function.

hog cycle is well known and is observed in every country to have a periodic recurrence of three or four years. Till now, this cycle has been attributed to market causes, to the periodic change in pork and fodder prices. However, it has been shown by recent research[11] that the hog cycle prevails also in non-market economies, for example in the communes of China or in the case of pigs reared by the poorer economic groups in India which are never sold in the market. It is therefore reasonable to assume that the hog cycle has an ecological basis which, under market conditions, entails the corresponding fluctuations in the prices of pork and maize.

The gestation period is 114–116 days and the reproductive age is reached in about one-and-a-half years. However, porkers are usually slaughtered before they are one year old. From these data the duration of the hog cycle is computed as $T = 2 \pi \sqrt{115 \times 300}$ days $= 1167$ days $= 3.2$ years in the case of intensive breeding. In the case of less intensive breeding the hog cycle will be prolonged and in the case of semi-domestication it may reach $T = 2 \pi \sqrt{115 \times 550}$ days $= 1580$ days $= 4.3$ years. It is revealing that in less developed countries the observed cycle is somewhat longer while in large-scale production the cycle may be reduced to $T = 2 \pi \sqrt{115 \times 200} = 952$ days $= 2.6$ years.

The empirical evidence of the hog cycle is adequately approximated by the formula. Let us compute the length of the cycle in the case of cattle. The gestation period is about 0.8 year and the average life expectancy is 1.5 years if the purpose is meat production. This yields an ecologic cycle of $T = 2 \pi \sqrt{0.8 \times 1.5}$ year $= 6.8$ years which is fairly close to observed data. Of course if cattle are used for draught then the cycle period will greatly increase together with its expected life-span and, for example, in India, where the cow is sacred and seldom slaughtered, the expected cycle length will be as long as fourteen to fifteen years.

So, life is unmistakably cyclical in the world of animals: propagation and procreation rates are always fluctuating and it is natural that this fluctuation is governed by the fundamental biological constants,

[11] See Gabor Kornai: 'An Econometric Model of the Hog Cycle in Hungary'. KOPINT, 1979.

the specific gestation period and the similarly specific ageing process (although humans are able to shorten the latter by taming and breeding). Consequently, cyclical growth is a basic law of life and the market cycle or the cycle exhibited by a planned economy is merely a special manifestation of this most primary form of motion in these specific systems of production. Economic historians have proved the existence of cycles even in pre-capitalistic economic formations. Perhaps the oldest written record of this is the well-known riddle in the Bible about the seven fat and seven lean cows. This enigma was solved for the Pharaoh by Joseph, who deserves credit for his pioneering anti-cyclic policy.

If life on this globe is chilly today and hot tomorrow, does this mean that it must remain this way? Are we for ever precluded from transcending the standard of the flock of zebras in recognizing and making the best of the true laws of our economic processes? I hope we are not. It is always possible to compute the equilibrium solution in the context of a given model. This solution is, of course, not suitable for direct use because it remains a rough sketch of a real equilibrium. But it may be possible to utilize the mathematical idea of the computation itself, the algorithm, spelling out where to start, what operations to perform, how the result is obtained and how its precision can be refined.

If any existing economic mechanism can be mirrored by mathematical equations and computational processes and if, by doing so, all the trends triggered by any given mechanism can be described and analysed, then the reverse must also be possible. A given, functional and adequate mathematical algorithm can be translated into an economic mechanism. But it is not enough to stipulate the conduct expected from the agents of the economy; they must also be motivated to act in a correct and purposeful manner that will secure equilibrium.

I am not sure whether it is possible to solve the treble task of translation, stipulation and motivation, nor can one see all the new problems arising in the course of propounding a solution. Nevertheless, the challenge to try is tempting. A solution, if it exists, must be surely far better than the current rules of the economic game and it will resemble neither market nor planning. Alas, the idea of a solution is not yet a solution—and a solution is not yet practical, even if it is faultless. Appreciating the usual time span required for translating scientific ideas and findings into practice, the survival of the old forms of motion in this millennium can be taken for granted. Therefore the practical implications of the cyclic movement will be the subject of the last section.

Cycles Within Cycles

Using the formula already applied successfully for ecological systems, let us examine a few major economic cycles.

In the temperate zone the period of agricultural production compasses the succession of the four seasons and its duration is one year. In olden times every country had to produce its 'daily bread'. However, as there was only one crop of grain a year, they had to store enough to last till the next harvest. The average stock was therefore about half a year's production, or let us assume somewhat more because of the requirement of seeds and growth. Therefore if $g = 1$ and $b = 0.6$, these values yield an agricultural cycle $T = 2 \pi \sqrt{0.6} = 4.9$ or, rounded up, 5 years. And, indeed, agricultural statistics usually reckoned with a 5-year moving average in order to present a clear trend of the strongly fluctuating production. This way the cyclic fluctuations were eliminated and the trend of real growth could be fairly well estimated.

It must be noted here that the agricultural cycle did run for a long time on nearly the same wave-length as the industrial cycle which emerged with industrialization, though not necessarily in unison with it due to its somewhat deviating length. The wave-length of the business cycle is formed in a different manner. If a 3-year term is accepted to be the value of capital intensity (this figure was shown to be an acceptable average for the past two centuries) and bearing in mind that unfinished and semi–finished stocks as well as the stock of unaccomplished investments correspond to 10 to 20 per cent of total production (meaning that the weighted average of production periods amounts to 35 to 70 days), the period will be $T = 2 \pi \sqrt{1095 \times 50}$ days = 1470 days = 4.03 years. This is in agreement with the average length observed in capitalist countries.[12]

As market economies and planned economies use essentially the same technologies, their average capital intensities and average production periods match fairly closely. It is therefore no wonder that the average investment cycle is similarly about four years in planned economies.

It is most likely that the slightly slower and longer European cycles at the end of the nineteenth century were affected by the enormous railway construction projects. Because of their long gestation periods and high capital intensities they increased the average value of b and g and temporarily prolonged also the duration of the business cycles proportionally.

It is also clear that at the point where the agricultural cycle and the industrial cycle 'meet,' that is, if they turn into recession in unison, a 20-yearly occurrence, the recession will be particularly severe. The interference of these two cycles with slightly different wave-lengths yields a complex picture. As an illustration, a 4-year and a 5-year cycle will add up to the theoretical course shown in Figure 3, assuming that their amplitudes and weights are the same.

Of course, the cycle of modern agriculture or 'agro-business' does not show any resemblance to those ancient 5-year fluctuations any longer and its impact is also muted. The situation grows more

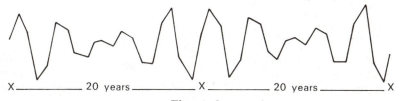

Figure 3

[12] The National Bureau of Economic Research, engaged chiefly in the analysis of business cycles, computed an average reference cycle of about 48 months, i.e., 4 years. For more detail see, e.g., F.C. Mills: *Price-Quantity Interaction in Business Cycles*. National Bureau of Economic Research. New York, 1946, p. 10.

complex if both the amplitudes and the weights of sectors are different and their respective growth rates also differ, as usually happens in economic reality. A specific and characteristic cycle period pertains to each product and each sector (their recommended estimation must start from capital intensities and production periods) and as all these sectors and products are added up with weights varying with time, the compound movement of the economy will be very intricate. It is extremely difficult and almost impossible to derive any conclusion from the time series of aggregate production or of national income about the primary cycles that produce their special configuration. This would require a very long time series and very frequent measurements, something which is not yet feasible in economic science.

The only viable way seems to be to assume the existence of a given cycle period—on the basis of other considerations, calculated, for example, precisely from the gestation periods and capital intensities—and then test this assumption as a statistical hypothesis, accepting or rejecting it for a given time series.

Different cycles may exist for the same product in different countries. For example, the building cycle is quite different in Europe and in the United States. In Europe, homes are built with longer average gestation periods lasting up to one year. Durable, even indestructible, materials are used and the structures last 50–60 years. In these circumstances the cycle period will be over 40 years. In the United States of America, most family homes are wooden structures. They are built much faster than European ones and remain in use for a much shorter period. Reckoning with four months of building time and a life-span of 30 years, the building cycle will be around $T = 2\pi\sqrt{4 \times 360}$ months $= 238$ months $= 20$ years. These cycles are in agreement with evidence.

In the United States a special problem emerges: one of the major branches of the economy, the automobile industry, oscillates on the same wave-length as the business cycle. The life-span of cars is extremely short because corrosion resistance is deliberately neglected. The average life of a car is five years and as the introduction of assembly lines shortened the production period appreciably, it does not now require more than about a month for the raw material to be worked up into a finished car. The cycle length in the automobile industry is thus approximately $T = 2\pi\sqrt{5/12}$ years $= 4.06$ years. This in itself contributes to the aggravation of cyclic motion through the principle of resonance. The problems could be substantially alleviated if more durable cars were manufactured as in Europe and Japan.

Thus the 'business cycle' or, in other words, the general investment cycle, is not the single and exclusive source of trouble, although it is certainly the dominating one, subordinating shorter cycles to itself. But there will be products and sectors in the upward phase of their cycles even in times of the worst business crises and, similarly, the best prosperity is liable to shelter sectors that temporarily or steadily decline or decay. This makes it so terribly difficult to iron out the cycles through outside, state interference. The actual diagnosis at any moment of the state of affairs is not unambiguous in itself. Ten expert economists will express twenty opinions about the exact phase of the cycle which the economy is going through—whether recession will deepen further or it has reached its bottom; whether increasing contract orders in one sector or another are sure signs of a revival or just provisional plateaus before a new recession, and so on.

However, the most dangerous are those cycles to which we give no attention because they remain hidden below the surface, the most difficult ones being those originating from the ecological character of human systems.

The previous section dealt with the cyclic development of species. Once it was found that the law of propagation of each is cyclic and the cycle is governed by the biological parameters (gestation period and predictable life-span) one could not but ask why mankind shouldn't share this destiny.

The human gestation period is clearly set at nine months. Life expectancy has increased with improving health care and may be estimated now to be around 60 years. In the advanced countries it is longer while in under-developed ones it is still far below this value.

Purely theoretically, these two figures yield a cycle period of

$T = 2 \pi \cdot \sqrt{0.75 \times 60}$ years = 42 years and may reach as far as $T = 2 \pi$ $\sqrt{0.75 \times 75}$ years = 47 years, that is, nearly half a century, with a 75-year life expectancy in Europe and the advanced western countries. After the Second World War life expectancy was only 30 years in the under-developed countries and in medieval Europe it was probably not much longer. This yields a cycle period of $T = 2 \pi$ $\sqrt{0.75 \times 30}$ years = 30 years.

Do we observe such a long ecological cycle in reality; is it possible to observe it and to feel its impact? It is probably not observed directly because not more than one such cycle can be noticed by an individual. Even if his life is deeply affected, because of the lack of recurrence he will not recognize the law but will only have the feeling of having had a unique life which he shares only with his contemporaries, saying, for example: 'After the war life got better and better; then came troubles and difficulties. I had hoped for something better, but now I only wish to live my old age in peace.' Or, quoting a 'cross-generation': 'My early years were incredibly difficult, my parents were bankrupt and each morning I had to deliver newspapers. But I gathered all my strength; I went to school and did my best, and you can see what I have achieved: everything here is mine, the fruit of my own work and I leave a big and influential family behind me.'

Similar cycles of long durations were first noticed by N.D. Kondratiev[13] when analyzing long-range price trends. The scientific echo of his discovery also reflects a long cycle very similar to the one he studied. After the crisis of the thirties there was a rather broad interest in his theory; his paper was translated into English[14] and his hypotheses were scrutinized by many but there was no universal agreement concerning them. The cycle was perhaps most firmly advocated by Schumpeter and Burns. Kondratiev's arguments were accepted and used also by a few Marxist economists, but the statistical evidence was not convincing and a satisfactory theoretical under-

[13] N.D. Kondratiev: 'Die Langen Wellen der Konjunktur'. *Archiv fur Sozial-wissenschaft und Sozialpolitik*, 1926, Vol. 56, pp. 573–609.

[14] 'The Long Waves in Economic Life'. *Review of Economic Statistics*, 1935, Vol. 17, pp. 105–15.

pinning concerning the mechanism of such long cycles was missing. After a while economic literature abandoned the theory, as it had so many other fashionable subjects, and left the discussions inconclusive.

However, after an interval roughly equivalent to a Kondratiev cycle, the problem reappeared and professional interest is again visibly growing. Since that time statistical data and time series have become longer and, let us hope, more accurate and, therefore, the statistical 'verification process' could be repeated. But a little hitch arose in the meantime: price statistics, which had always provided the most convincing evidence of the existence of Kondratiev cycles, showed that since the thirties there has been an almost permanent inflation, and thus the regularities of the longer range are buried and obscured.

Most typically, in one single publication[15] and on basis of essentially identical data, the existence of the cycle was rejected and accepted by two equally careful and outstanding Dutch professors—A. van der Zwan of Rotterdam, and J.J. van Duijn of Delft respectively—substantially on the ground of a periodicity derived from the works of Kondratiev and Schumpeter, and later of Burns and Mitchell:[16]

	Beginning	Peak	End	Duration
First cycle	1793	1815	1849	56 years
Second cycle	1849	1873	1896	47 years
Third cycle	1896	1920	1938	42 years

I believe the third cycle may have lasted until the middle or end of the Second World War—it is impossible to state the exact turning point anyway—and the fourth cycle, after peaking around the late sixties and taking a down-turn in the seventies, became an important reason for our present growth difficulties.

The working of the cycle was explained as an ecologic fluctuation of the human species and is consequently of a demographic nature which must manifest itself in demographic data. This way the

[15] S.K. Kuipers and G.J. Lanjouw (ed.): *Prospects of Economic Growth*. North Holland. Amsterdam, 1980.

[16] W.C. Mitchell: *Measuring Business Cycles*. National Bureau of Economic Research. New York, 1946, Table 165.

Second World War, with its sizeable genocides and the explosive birth rates experienced everywhere in its aftermath, was a natural starting point of a demographic wave.

This is the point where demography gives a helping hand because, probably never thinking about the Kondratiev cycles or any other theory of long economic waves, it finds long-term fluctuations in birth rates. These are called Easterlin cycles after the scholar who discovered them.[17] As far as I know, the intimate relation between the Easterlin cycles and the Kondratiev cycles has not so far been noted. However, the great mathematical demographer, N. Keyfitz, gives the following explanation for the emergence of the Easterlin cycles:[18]

The high United States fertility of the 1950s and subsequent decline has puzzled observers. It could not be due to prosperity, since income in the 1950s was not as high as in the 1960s. That children are positively related to income in time series did not seem to help here, until Richard Easterlin (1961, 1968) noted that the prosperity of couples of child-bearing age is what we should look for, not general prosperity. He pointed out that [in the case of] couples of child-bearing age in the 1950s, born between the humps of the 1920s and the 1940s, not only would their promotion be relatively rapid, but in any one position, in so far as there is age-complementarity in production, they would frequently have the advantage of meeting situations in which they were too few to do the necessary work, with resulting appreciation of their services. This would often be expressed in material terms and would result in high wages and good prospects relative to what people of their age would be paid in a different age configuration, and they would have a sense of security and well-being. Their confidence is well-founded, for they will spend

[17] R.A. Easterlin: 'The Baby Boom in Perspective'. *American Economic Review*. 1961, Vol. 51, pp. 869–911. 'Does Human Fertility Adjust to the Environment?' *American Economic Review*. 1971, Vol. 61, pp. 399–407.

[18] N. Keyfitz: 'Population Waves' in T.N.E. Greville (ed.): *Population Dynamics*. Academic Press. New York, 1972.

their whole working lives in the same advantageous position. They translate their advantage into child-bearing, perhaps projecting their security into the next generation and feeling that their children will be in demand just as they are. So strong was this effect in the 1950s that it entirely reversed the tendency of the classical demographic model with fixed age-specific rates. Instead of a dip echoing the dip of the 1930s, the 1950s showed fertility at the highest level in half a century. The 1930s gave a relative advantage to their children by producing few of them, and these later repaid the advantage by having more children. Such a mechanism could produce a very stable result if the rise in birth rates was of just the right amount to compensate for the few parents. In the actual case the rise over-compensated; the number of parents in the 1950s may have been ten per cent under trend, while birth rates were twenty per cent over trend.

The subsequent steady fall of the birth rate in the 1960s may well be due to the entry into child-bearing ages of the large cohorts born in the 1940s. If this is the dominant mechanism operating, we can predict continued low birth rates at least through the 1970s. Not until about 1990 will the parental generation again be small enough to be encouraged to have large families. Instead of the waves of generation length in the free response of the demographic model we find waves two generations in length.

The demographer was quoted *in extenso* because he gave a clear presentation of what was said in the previous chapter about the mechanism of the cycle and also illumined the inter-dependence of human ecology and the economic environment.

If the birth rate fluctuates (as it actually does) the age structure of the population will also fluctuate. There will be times when relatively more people are actively working and they must support relatively few infants and pensioners. And, again, there will be times when relatively more will have to be supported by the working population: a mass of youth going to school and old people who have retired. It could be also said or imagined that the 'capital intensity' of the reproduction of the human race is fluctuating. There are periods when schooling and the provision of pensions are not a problem, and the rate of economic development is rocketing. It gives the impression that it would be possible to provide more and better schools and much higher pensions, and the statesmen usually yield to the pressure and enact a 'great society'. But 'ups' are necessarily followed by 'downs' with a lag of 20 to 25 years. The relative number of students and pensioners increases and the accumulated funds are found to be insufficient. The state faces the menace of going bankrupt and statesmen set themselves the task of going back on their promises and codified statutes by way of crooked reasoning and all sorts of circumlocution.

Demography has an exact indicator for the description of this symptom: the 'dependency rate'. The figure in the numerator of the dependency rate is the number of people below and above working age while its denominator shows the number of the active population, carrying the former 'on their shoulders'. Irrespective of the country for which I investigated its trend—be it Hungary, the United States, the Soviet Union or India—this ratio displayed the same typical fluctuation of a 40–50-year cycle length, indicating that 'uniform age distribution' is the same master dream for demographers as is economic equilibrium for economists or female faithfulness in Mozart's *Cosi Fan Tutte*: 'Here and there you/Hear about it/But where can it be?/It is nowhere/It is nowhere. But if faithfulness is theoretically non-existent, the notion of unfaithfulness cannot be defined either, because it may be only appreciated as the lack of faithfulness. As long as we do not know where to find equilibrium we cannot find any measure of fluctuation, which is so badly needed for the purpose of foresight. Our ignorance in all these most human fields—economy, demography and the relations of sexes—puts us to shame.

Actual statistical data are only suitable for a very uncertain estimation of the length of the Kondratiev cycle. First of all, accuracy would require long and homogeneous time series encompassing not less than two or three complete cycles. Such homogeneous time series for 100–150 years are not, and will probably never, be available. Methods of statistical measurement change along with science and with the development of record keeping. Data of bygone stages do not lend themselves readily to being subjected retrospectively to the supposedly more exact process of measurement now in use or to be used in the future.

Even if there existed such a time series, adequate in evey respect and of suitable length, or if it could be devised in the future, it would be still difficult to distinguish the components of growth and long-range fluctuation. Harmonic analysis, the breaking-down of a time series into its cyclic components, is elaborated with the necessary rigor only for stationary time series. Applying this theory to the series showing exponential growth will bias the results: either the rate of actual growth will be under-estimated by attributing an exaggerated weight to the cyclic component or, contrariwise, a higher growth rate will be computed than the true value because of the under-estimated weight of the cyclic component.

It must be noted here that the existence of long cycles is disregarded in current statistical practice and here we have another source of over-estimation.

Instead of analysis, for the sake of a clear idea, one may consider and even calculate the modification of the observed long-range rate of growth of the economy if a Kondratiev cycle of a given weight is super-imposed upon this exponential growth.

Let us assume that the long-range rate of growth is equal to the average annual growth of about 2.5 per cent claimed for the last fifty years in advanced countries. By adding a very mild Kondratiev component of a weight of a paltry 2 per cent to this it will be found that, at the peak of the boom, the rate of growth reaches 4.5 per cent, while at the bottom of the Kondratiev cycle the rate of growth falls to 0.5 per cent. A slightly more powerful Kondratiev cycle of 2.5 per cent weight is enough to extinguish the rate of growth and to induce all the syndromes of stagnation especially because, in addition to other cycles of lesser importance, the usual business cycle must also be added to the former two factors, with its variable but pretty considerable weight.

The behavior of the business cycle in the upward and in the

downward phase of the Kondratiev cycle is particularly important because it exhibits a qualitative change. If the Kondratiev cycle is strong enough then, in alliance with the long-range rate of growth, it may balance the descending phase of the business cycle and thereby it can minimize all the symptoms connected with the down-swing of the business cycle. In such cases no recession and especially no crisis is manifest. Although there will be a bit of temporary slackening, production will soon gather speed again. The business cycle carried on the back of the upward Kondratiev cycle will show long booms and very short and mild slack periods. This is the stage when economists and statesmen are apt to completely forget about cycles or boast about having overcome them. The economy is in full blast and the cycle is 'obsolete'.[19] This euphoric approach was typical of the 1960s and of the postwar years of 'economic wonders,' later unmasked as periods of recovery.

The case is different in the declining phase of the Kondratiev cycle. If the Kondratiev component is strong enough it is able to reverse the qualitative course of business cycles. Recession will be replaced by crises, production and national income drops, negative rates of growth reappear, depression is prolonged and, after relatively brief revival periods, considered 'incomplete;' stagnation, recession, even crises are the order of the day.

This latter description is a fair portrayal of the situation prevailing at the end of the seventies. It may be therefore supposed that the new quality of business cycles can be traced back to the existence of a moderately heavy Kondratiev cycle.

If all this is true, and there seems to be ample evidence to support it, then the present generally critical period, reminding us of the early 1920s and 30s, will persist and the crisis will further deepen in the eighties and nineties.[20] The advent of a new upswing can be

---

[19] This characteristic illusion was criticized in the title of the volume edited by Bronfenbrenner: *Is the Business Cycle Obsolete?* Wiley. New York, 1969.

[20] The general crisis of the 1930s was not simply a 'general crisis of capitalism'. It is now known that at the end of the thirties the rate of growth decelerated markedly in the Soviet Union also. This internal crisis was indicated also by the stepped-up collectivization and the construction trials.

anticipated only about the turn of the millennium, when the new Kondratiev cycle will surge again, with the arc of world economy on its crest.[21]

At this point and in conclusion, let me stress what I believe to be the most important point about the Kondratiev cycle. While hog cycles or agricultural and even business cycles have proved to be more or less 'local' cycles of a limited range and concerning only one country or a small group of countries, the Kondratiev cycle has functioned from the outset as a universal *world* economic cycle. Naturally, business cycles always did and do cause strong 'resonance' in all the markets maintaining commercial relations with the country in question. All the same, the short-term business cycle of 4–5 years never totally synchronized with the economic fluctuations of the advanced capitalist countries. Although it is admitted that perfectly opposite phases were not exhibited by history—that is, none of the slump periods of, say, Britain coincided with the prosperity of, say, France or Germany—still there has always been some displacement between peaks or troughs, a half year or a whole year or even more in favor of one country or another.

The only case known to sweep the capitalist world with devastating simultaneity was the crisis of the 1930s when, along with other coincidences, the down-swing of an agricultural, a building, a business and a Kondratiev cycle joined forces. And I strongly suspect that the synchronizing force, the 'conductor,' was the Kondratiev cycle.

The Kondratiev cycle seems to be *ab ovo* a world symptom. Considering that the world economy itself can be considered to have taken shape and become fully inter-connected only since the turn of this century (when the final allocation of the inhabited world among the leading powers was accomplished) and given the growing involvement of world economy, the role of the Kondratiev cycle can be expected to grow.

The wave of crisis of the years 1974-75 might not have been as deep and powerful as the one of 1929–33, but it surely affected many

---

[21] It was seen that the demographic forecast of Keyfitz similarly predicts a change just before the millennium.

more people. In the 40 years between the two crises enormous new masses of people and even whole continents joined the system of commodity production, that is, became part of a world economic system in the stricter sense. The self-sufficient people of Africa, Asia and the South Sea Islands who did not produce commodities for the market felt the 1930 crisis most indirectly, if at all. However, the crisis of the mid-seventies demonstrated to all people around the globe and in a most direct manner that even the most advanced countries, the top powers, are helpless and unable to secure an undisturbed daily life. Let us not neglect the vast wave of disappointment and bitterness arising out of this historical experience. And the worst is yet to come: the great crisis of the 1930s will predictably have to repeat itself generations later, in the 1980s.

Conclusion

If the ideas and theories presented in this book are correct, we must be prepared for a deceleration of growth and universal stagnation of economies in the coming period of about twenty years, that is, until the opening of the second millennium. In this context, all the strains originating from the high proportion of the younger and older age groups—those not actively employed and the unemployable—will be demographically most acute, especially in the problems of education, training and the provision of old-age pensions. The short-term economic cycle with a 4 to 5 year period will take on a new shape, prosperity will be brief and incomplete while recessions will be deep and critical.

Gloomy times are to come. When and where the lightning will come from the whirl of clouds is unknown to the most excellent meteorologist: he can only forecast the storm.

There isn't much to do about it. Neither the demographic age structure nor the value judgements of society can be transformed and, even if they could be, it would be a further 20 or 30 years before the transformation bears fruit. Therefore an uneasy feeling of impotence and disillusionment will necessarily prevail.

If the term '*mal du siecle*' was coined for the disposition prevailing at the end of the nineteenth century (a disposition having very similar economic reasons) then we now face the troubles of the '*mal du millennaire*' and the occasional slivers of hope and optimism will be scant and few. The situation is worse than it was at the turn of the century because we seem to have come to the end of our tether: we are chewing at the kernel of time.

If we are able to rise above the horizon of our own generation we may still harbor some serene optimism: all the listed troubles carry their own remedies...but it is a long road to recovery and it is a rather distant comfort to await the new millennium, bringing along its own prosperity.

I strongly doubt that in the new millennium we will be able to arrive at the society of scientists which Plato pictured so captivatingly. But Marxism already has declared its theory, against its own practice: politics as servant to science. Maybe in the new millennium we will come one step nearer to this goal.

This already implies some ethical guidance concerning our conduct and activity: having realized the true course of events and hence our true interests, we must not exacerbate these troubles by short-sighted demographic and economic interference chasing the phantoms of maximal growth which are for ever slipping away. Let us rather seek harmony.

Index

About the Author

Andrew Brody is Scientific Adviser, Institute of Economics, Hungarian Academy of Sciences. He holds degrees in mathematics, economics, and industrial economics. He has taught and lectured at the Institute of Technology, Budapest; Harvard University; University of Zambia; Institute for Economic Analysis, New York University; Battelle Laboratories (Columbus); and the Institute for Economic Growth (Delhi). In addition to SLOWDOWN: GLOBAL ECONOMIC MALADIES (an earlier version was published in Hungary in 1983 under the title SLOW DOWN: ABOUT OUR ECONOMIC MALADIES), Dr. Brody is the author of PRO-PORTIONS, PRICES AND PLANNING, and (in Hungarian) of CYCLES AND CONTROLS and CAPITAL INTENSITY OF PRODUCTION IN CAPITALISM. He is also the co-author (with A. Carter) of three books in English on input/output analysis. Dr. Brody is a fellow of the Econometric Society, as well as a member of the Association of Mathematical Economists, and the Association Scientifique Européenne D'Economie Appliquée.